Foucault ⅄ ⅄ity Volume I,
▲ ⅃nowledge

Edinburgh Philosophical Guides Series

Titles in the series include:

Kant's *Critique of Pure Reason*
Douglas Burnham with Harvey Young

Derrida's *Of Grammatology*
Arthur Bradley

Heidegger's *Being and Time*
William Large

Plato's *Republic*
D. J. Sheppard

Spinoza's *Ethics*
Beth Lord

Descartes' *Meditations on First Philosophy*
Kurt Brandhorst

Nietzsche's *Thus Spoke Zarathustra*
Douglas Burnham and Martin Jesinghausen

Deleuze's *Difference and Repetition*
Henry Somers-Hall

Foucault's *History of Sexuality Volume I, The Will to Knowledge*
Mark Kelly

Kant's *Groundwork of the Metaphysics of Morals*
John Callanan

Visit the Edinburgh Philosophical Guides Series website at www.
euppublishing.com/series/edpg

Foucault's
History of Sexuality Volume I,
The Will to Knowledge

An Edinburgh Philosophical Guide

Mark G. E. Kelly

EDINBURGH
University Press

© Mark G. E. Kelly, 2013

Edinburgh University Press Ltd
22 George Square, Edinburgh EH8 9LF

www.euppublishing.com

Typeset in 11/13pt Monotype Baskerville
by Servis Filmsetting Ltd, Stockport, Cheshire, and
printed and bound in Great Britain by
CPI Group (UK) Ltd, Croydon CR0 4YY

A CIP record for this book is available from the British Library

ISBN 978 0 7486 4890 0 (hardback)
ISBN 978 0 7486 4889 4 (paperback)
ISBN 978 0 7486 4891 7 (webready PDF)
ISBN 978 0 7486 8035 1 (epub)
ISBN 978 0 7486 8036 8 (Amazon ebook)

The right of Mark G. E. Kelly
to be identified as author of this work
has been asserted in accordance with
the Copyright, Designs and Patents Act 1988.

Contents

Series Editor's Preface

To us, the principle of this series of books is clear and simple: what readers new to philosophical classics need first and foremost is help with *reading* these key texts. That is to say, help with the often antique or artificial style, the twists and turns of arguments on the page, as well as the vocabulary found in many philosophical works. New readers also need help with those first few daunting and disorienting sections of these books, the points of which are not at all obvious. The books in this series take you through each text step-by-step, explaining complex key terms and difficult passages which help to illustrate the way a philosopher thinks in prose.

We have designed each volume in the series to correspond to the way the texts are actually taught at universities around the world, and have included helpful guidance on writing university-level essays or examination answers. Designed to be read alongside the text, our aim is to enable you to *read* philosophical texts with confidence and perception. This will enable you to make your own judgements on the texts, and on the variety of opinions to be found concerning them. We want you to feel able to join the great dialogue of philosophy, rather than remain a well-informed eavesdropper.

Douglas Burnham

Acknowledgements

I want to thank Carol Macdonald, my editor at EUP, for her helpfulness and supportiveness. I thank Stephanie Deuchar for patient comments on the early parts of the book, and Jessica Whyte for helpful feedback on the later parts.

I also thank John Attridge, who kindly let me use his vacant seaside flat as a hermitage to write significant portions of this book.

I would like to acknowledge Stella Sandford, who, when I began teaching at Middlesex, thoughtfully suggested swapping modules so that I could teach one that included *The Will to Knowledge* as a set text, which experience led me to write this book, and for other forms of professional encouragement and example.

Note on Texts

An Introduction, vol. I of *The History of Sexuality*, trans. Robert Hurley (New York: Pantheon, 1978). Reprinted as *The Will to Knowledge* (London: Penguin, 1998). Originally published as *La Volonté de savoir (Histoire de la sexualité 1)* (Paris: Gallimard, 1976).

Title

This is a guidebook to the first volume of Michel Foucault's *History of Sexuality*, which he called *The Will to Knowledge* (*La Volonté de savoir*). The book has not generally been known by this title in English, however. It was first translated under the title *The History of Sexuality Volume I: An Introduction*, which it still bears in North America. Since 1998, though, one British edition published by Penguin has been titled *The Will to Knowledge*. In every respect other than the cover and frontispiece, all English editions are identical: the content and pagination are the same, being a translation from the French by Robert Hurley.

I prefer the title of *The Will to Knowledge*, and will generally use it to refer to the text in what follows. The subtitle *An Introduction* was first used because Foucault initially did intend the first volume to serve as the introduction to his *History of Sexuality*. However, that project did not unfold as he initially planned: it took longer, and changed form, such that the first volume is no introduction to what comes later.

Translation

Robert Hurley's translation of the book, used in all editions, is highly readable, but not without faults. To an extent, it prioritises literary style over technical accuracy. Since so many are familiar with his phrasing,

I retain it where I think it works, but frequently find it inadequate and provide my own alternatives.

Throughout this guidebook, I provide page references to *The Will to Knowledge* in parentheses. These consist of the page number in Hurley's English translation, followed by a slash, then the page number in the French original. Where I have used my own translation, I add an asterisk (*) to the reference to indicate this; otherwise, quotations are to the published translation.

Hurley's translation is in American English, hence so are quotations from it. The rest of the book, including my translations, uses British orthography. A similar distinction is observed in relation to the words 'biopolitics' and 'biopower'. While Foucault always in *The Will to Knowledge* writes 'bio-politics' and 'bio-power', with a hyphen, the hyphen has mostly been dropped in subsequent uses, so I too will dispense with it in my own usage.

Introduction

I will begin with a confession: *The Will to Knowledge* changed my life. I first encountered Foucault as a philosophy student in the late nineties. Foucault was really on the edge of what was acceptable in philosophy at that time; indeed, this has changed little today. Despite that Foucault is now the most cited single author in the humanities, philosophy, his native discipline, has remained largely hostile to him.

The few lectures on Foucault at the end of my final year were for me the most exciting of the degree, the ideas vertiginous, seeming to turn all received philosophical opinion on its head. I went away determined to learn more about him. The first book I read in this endeavour happened to be *The Will to Knowledge*. I don't think I could have picked a better one.

The Will to Knowledge is an exciting book. It is short and readable, at least by the standards of philosophical masterworks – and I believe it is such a work. The topics Foucault deals with in this book – sex and power – are immediately relevant to all readers and combine to make it exceptionally interesting. On both topics, Foucault overturns all previous wisdom. Regarding sex, he claims that it is an artificial construct imposed by power on our bodies and pleasures, rather than something natural that we need to liberate. Regarding power, Foucault claims that it is not essentially repressive, but something essentially productive, to be found everywhere in our lives and in our society, affecting and being produced in each everyday thing we do (including sex) in ways we do not understand and scarcely suspect.

The material on sex interested me for reasons that Foucault adequately explains in the book itself: we live in a sex-obsessed culture. But the real shock was what he had to say about power. I think this is in fact the most important part of the book from the point of view of the history of ideas, and one which for all Foucault's celebrity has yet to be properly processed. His thoughts about sex, which take up the bulk of his book, do have far-ranging implications for our society. However, his insights in relation to power have implications that range further still, which apply to all societies, and all facets of them moreover, not only to sex and sexuality. Foucault became a growing preoccupation for me from then on. Within eighteen months, I was proposing to write a PhD thesis on his thought, which in turn became my first book, *The Political Philosophy of Michel Foucault*.

Few will be as taken with *The Will to Knowledge* as I was, but it has had a broad impact, as a major event in the history of thought. In the three and a half decades since its publication, it has made an immense impact. It has spawned entire fields, specifically queer theory and the sexuality studies. It has changed more lives than just mine: a mere three-word phrase from the book is the basis of an autobiographical meditation by feminist philosopher Ladelle McWhorter, *Bodies and Pleasures*, which is itself longer than Foucault's original book, detailing McWhorter's attempt to think through these words in her own life.

For all that, Foucault's book remains underexplored. The secondary texts that engage with it are rife with misunderstandings. I do not mean to castigate the commentators unduly, however. Foucault's book is subtly difficult, with nuances he does not spell out. No matter how many times I read it, I still find passages that surprise me.

Structure

The structure of *The Will to Knowledge* is not particularly clear and can be confusing. It is set out in five 'parts', and some of these parts are sub-divided into multiple 'chapters'. In this guidebook, I will simply follow Foucault's structure in order to make it easy to relate this guide to the primary text.

The English edition, like the French original (but unlike the editions in some other languages), begins directly with Part One, without any preface. This part of the book sets out what Foucault is arguing against (what he calls 'the repressive hypothesis') and why. There are three distinct moments here. From pages 1 to 6 in the English, Foucault sets out the repressive hypothesis. From pages 6 to 8 he then goes on to criticise it, before in pages 8 to 13 foregrounding the methodology for the rest of the book.

Next comes Foucault's own history of sexuality. This is, unsurprisingly, the largest component of his book, comprising more than half of its length. As it is more straightforward than other elements of Foucault's book, we spend somewhat less time on it than he does: dealing with this accounts for approximately one third of this guidebook. This historical segment comprises Parts Two and Three of *The Will to Knowledge*, as well as the third and fourth chapters of Part Four.

The first and second chapters of Part Four, however, represent a significant digression. Though there is no indication of this in their chapter titles, these two chapters of *The Will to Knowledge* are where Foucault propounds his new way of understanding power.

The final part of the book, Part Five, comprises two main moments. Firstly, Foucault introduces a concept he calls 'bio-power'. From page 135 to page 145 in the English translation, he sets out what this means, and he then applies this concept to his understanding of sexuality between pages 145 and 150. He then changes tack, leaving a blank line in the middle of a page to signal this, to the consideration of the nature of sex and sexuality from pages 150 to 157. He ends Part Five with his conclusion to the whole book, from pages 157 to 159. I deal with these sections in the same order Foucault presents them.

Foucault's book thus basically comprises five elements: (1) the critique of the repressive hypothesis; (2) the genealogy of sexuality; (3) the reconception of power; (4) the analysis of biopower; (5) the critique of the ontology of sex.

1. Historical Context

Biographical Sketch

Michel Foucault (1926–84) was one of the most prominent French thinkers of the late twentieth century, a period of extraordinary fecundity in French thought. As such, he has been one of the greatest influences on the contemporary humanities and social sciences since the 1970s worldwide.

Foucault was in some ways part of the French establishment: a child of the professional middle class, he was educated at France's most elite undergraduate institution, the École normale supérieure, seemed to follow every turn in intellectual fashion, and was elected to France's most prestigious academic institution, the Collège de France. In many ways, however, he was an outsider: a homosexual, who spent much of his adult life in a self-imposed academic exile outside France, whose work flouted disciplinary conventions; a convert to political activism in his later years, who fought police and submitted to arrest, and whose untimely death from AIDS has fed salacious, slanderous rumours.

Foucault's work can be understood as falling into several distinct periods, although one should not take this to imply wholesale changes in his position, but rather only shifts in his interests and understanding. He himself understood his career towards its end as having always been an investigation of the relation between subjectivity, politics and truth. Certainly, *The Will to Knowledge* can be understood as part of such a project.

His earliest work, in the 1950s, was concerned with psychology and largely followed the dominant intellectual tendencies of the day, Marxism, psychoanalysis and existential phenomenology. This reflected his education: he had attended lectures by the phenomenologist Maurice Merleau-Ponty, as a student at the École normale supérieure been mentored by the Marxist philosopher Louis Althusser and briefly joined the French Communist Party, and then pursued studies in psychology.

Foucault was to exclude this early work from his canon later, seeing his career as really beginning with his doctoral thesis, the *History of Madness*, published in 1961. It represents the outgrowth of his earlier psychological works, now defining his own distinctive position in relation to madness rather than following others. This position is, in short, that the modern West has excluded madness as part of a valorisation of 'rational' thinking, and excluded the mad in the process. This book set the pattern for several of Foucault's books, including *The Will to Knowledge*: it is a 'history of the present', in which the historical roots of contemporary thought and practices are sought. It also sets the pattern for *The Will to Knowledge* by challenging the French academic orthodoxies of Marxism and psychoanalysis in particular (he challenges the orthodoxy of phenomenology too, but much more subtly and implicitly, and we will not look at it in what follows).

His next book was a tangent from the history of madness, relating to it inasmuch as the persecution of madness has been conducted through medical institutions: this was a history of modern medicine, *The Birth of the Clinic*, published in 1963. There was a change in this work not explained by the shift in subject matter, however, announced in its preface though not really followed through in its content. This was a new methodology, clearly influenced by what is often called French 'structuralism'. Though Foucault did not like that term, he clearly at this time fitted into what was popularly understood by the word, proposing to pay intense attention to language and its structures.

The method was implemented more fully in his next book, *The Order of Things*, published in 1966. Like his previous books, this was a historical work, but one entirely concerned with discourse, and no longer with social or institutional change. Rather, this book charts certain widespread changes that have occurred at particular times in modernity across the 'human sciences'. This book was a huge, but unexpected, success because of its sensational concluding claims that current forms of humanist knowledge were perhaps about to disappear in the face of structuralism, securing Foucault's name as a major philosopher. He followed this work up with an introspective meditation on language, *The Archaeology of Knowledge*, which appeared in 1969.

Through the 1960s, Foucault saw himself as developing a methodology he called 'archaeology', of uncovering the buried layers beneath our discourses. Now, however, his trajectory shifted. Much was happening to Foucault at this time. In 1968 there had been a major political crisis in France, the 'events' of May, in which students and then workers had seriously threatened to overthrow the government. Foucault returned to Paris from Tunis, where he had been living and working, in the immediate aftermath of this. While the 1968 revolt was abortive, the atmosphere of tumult and rebellion continued for many years. Foucault had never been particularly politically active before, even when in the Communist Party, but now threw himself into activism, more or less continuously from that point on till his death. He had returned to Paris charged with establishing the philosophy department at a new experimental university on the edge of Paris. He assembled and took charge of an extraordinarily radical set of teachers, including many of the biggest names of the next generation of French philosophy.

His research took a marked political turn. Little more than a year after returning to France, he was elected to the Collège de France, in 1970. A professorship at the Collège is the highest academic post in France, and is tenable for life. The only professional responsibility it carries is to give an annual series of lectures relating to one's work in progress. Foucault used his inaugural lecture at the Collège to announce a new methodology, 'genealogy'. This marked a shift from the pure study of discourse to the position that discourse can only be adequately understood by studying the institutional context of its production. He went on to write two books during the 1970s in this vein: *Discipline and Punish* (1975), and the subject of this guidebook, *The Will to Knowledge* (1976).

After this, he wrote two more books, the second and third volumes of *The History of Sexuality* series which *The Will to Knowledge* had inaugurated, both published on his deathbed in 1984. He had contracted AIDS sometime in the early eighties, before HIV had been identified as its cause. He thus died, aged 57, *The History of Sexuality* incomplete by at least one volume.

The History of *The History of Sexuality*

Foucault first started talking about doing a history of sexuality well before he actually began writing one. He mentions the project explicitly in his *Archaeology of Knowledge*,[1] published in 1969, and he was certainly interested in sexuality as a topic much earlier, saying a lot about it in particular in a 1963 piece, 'A Preface to Transgression'. Indeed, he claimed, albeit years after the fact, that at the time of his doctoral thesis, the *History of Madness*, published in 1961, he already had in mind a parallel study on sexuality.[2] We can trace things back still further: at his 1951 *agrégation* examination at the end of his time at the École normale, Foucault was randomly assigned the subject of 'sexuality', to which he apparently protested, since it was a topic that had never been set before and for which he was unprepared.[3] He was thus forced to look at sexuality intellectually, apparently for the first time.

That said, he must have encountered sexuality as a topic even before this. Sexuality was through most of the twentieth century – until Foucault wrote about it, in fact – a notion that was identified in theory with one figure, or at least one school, namely Freud and psychoanalysis. Freud had produced an explosive account of the workings of the human mind that placed sexuality at the core of our psychology and motivations. Specifically, Freud was inclined to diagnose the cause of mental problems in the repression of sexual feelings that were deemed inappropriate, particularly those towards one's parents. Although Freud was considered too avant-garde in Paris in the 1940s to figure on the university syllabus, students and intellectuals avidly read his works, and Foucault would certainly have been familiar with them as a student. Foucault would engage with psychoanalysis throughout *The Will to Knowledge*, albeit often not entirely explicitly, as the dominant theory of sexuality at the time he was writing.

There is a particular reason why Foucault may have been interested in sexuality as a topic, namely that he was gay, in the sense of being sexually attracted to other men. This might have provoked an interest in the topic, because homosexuality was severely stigmatised at the time, hence to be homosexual was to experience one's sexuality as problematic. Foucault rarely publicly announced his homosexuality, though he did talk about it to some extent, for example in a 1982 interview,[4] and he did describe himself as 'homosexual'.[5] However, he never 'came out' in the sense of making a deliberate, public act of self-identification as homosexual, despite that his partner Daniel Defert was open about his own homosexuality.[6] As we will see, Foucault was not keen on sexual categories.

This lack of identification would have done little to lessen the persecution Foucault experienced for his homosexuality, however. Throughout his youth, homosexuality was illegal for under-21s in France, and indecent exposure laws that targeted homosexuals for harsher punishment than others were introduced in 1960. Homosexuals were officially barred from working in the French educational system.[7] Although Foucault was clearly able to have a career despite this technicality, according to Didier Eribon, Foucault's homosexuality did result in his being blackballed for high office that he otherwise could have achieved in the French Ministry of Education.[8] Certainly, the categorisation by others as homosexual is something under which Foucault suffered. He claims his homosexuality led to his being marginalised in the Communist Party during his stint in that organisation.[9] It would seem that this discrimination played a role in his depression while a student in Paris,[10] and in his desire to leave France.[11] Leaving France, Foucault found himself in places where his homosexuality was if anything even more problematic. He was forced to leave his job in Poland because of the discovery of a homosexual liaison of his.[12] He was beaten in Tunis in connection with his homosexuality – although David Macey implies that Foucault was set up by the Tunisian authorities because of his nascent political activities.[13] It seems likely that these experiences would have been a considerable spur to thinking about the connection between power and sexuality. It might also have understandably influenced Foucault in his antipathy towards sexual categories.

Genealogy

Despite the long gestation of the idea of the project, the precise content of Foucault's study of sexuality was, however, unmistakably a product of the precise point of his career at which he wrote it. As his second, and last, full-scale 'genealogy', it represents a refinement of this method of study.

The development of genealogy had begun with Foucault's appointment to the Collège de France. Its development can be followed through the annual lectures he gave there. The first of these series, given in 1970, was entitled 'The Will to Knowledge' – that is, it had the very same title that he would later give to the first volume of *The History of Sexuality*. When it was published in French, it was therefore called *Leçons sur la volonté de savoir* – 'Lessons on the will to knowledge' – so as to avoid confusion with the first volume of *The History of Sexuality*; it still awaits publication in English. Foucault could not have foreseen this confusion, since he never intended for the lectures to be published.

The lectures corresponded more closely to the title than the later book does, since they focus on knowledge itself, rather than on sexuality. The title is drawn from the thought of German philosopher Friedrich Nietzsche, as is the term 'genealogy'. 'The will to knowledge' is not a particularly prominent concept in Nietzsche's thought, but it is a phrase that he uses in multiple works, and Foucault thinks its importance in Nietzsche has been underestimated. Where most readers of Nietzsche see it as a subordinate concept to the much more prominent notion of a 'will to power', Foucault thinks that Nietzsche moves from a concern with the will to knowledge in some of his books to one with the will to power in others.[14]

The full Nietzschean heritage of the notion of 'genealogy' was explored by Foucault in a 1971 essay, 'Nietzsche, Genealogy, History'. Nietzsche uses this term prominently in the title of one of his best-known works, *The Genealogy of Morality*. In this book, Nietzsche purports to trace a kind of secret history of morality. As he sees it, morality was invented by slaves to feel good about themselves by telling themselves that it was virtuous to suffer. Over time, slaves were able to use this story to gain power by convincing everyone that it was true. The slaves thus ended up as the masters, but unlike the previous, aristocratic rulers, the slaves pretended not to be masters, but rather continued to valorise victimhood in a hypocritical pose. Hence, for Nietzsche, morality, even though it appears to be opposed to self-interest and oppression, is in fact a tool of both. It is, for Nietzsche, like all things subservient to the principle of the will to power: it is invented as a ruse to gain power.

Foucault's allegiance to Nietzsche is not strict. Indeed, a strict allegiance to Nietzsche would be contradictory inasmuch as Nietzsche did not lay out a dogma he wanted others to follow. Foucault's allegiance to Nietzsche consists in a few key ways in which he broadly follows Nietzsche's method. The first of these is in Foucault's historical approach, where the Nietzschean influence is already prominent in the *History of Madness*. Foucault follows Nietzsche in looking for the genealogical traces of our contemporary social order in past events, and in using the description of these traces as a way of undermining and criticising the status quo. Foucault differs from Nietzsche, however, in doing history in a meticulously documentary way. Foucault is also much more ambivalent about our contemporary order than Nietzsche, who engages in a hyperbolic tirade against contemporary civilisation. Foucault does follow Nietzsche, however, secondly, in seeing truth as something constructed based on motivations, rather than something that simply gets to the underlying nature of things. Foucault also follows Nietzsche in giving prominence to the concept of power, though what Foucault takes power to be is rather different from Nietzsche's use of the term: where the latter understood power as an individual's impulse, a matter of 'will', Foucault understands power as a form of social relation. Foucault's invocation of 'will' in the 'will to knowledge' seems to be more emblematic than substantive.

In between the first Collège lecture series and the first volume of *The History of Sexuality*, Foucault gave five further annual lecture series. These form an important component of the background against which *The Will to Knowledge* should be understood. Two of these series, those of 1971–2 and 1972–3, remain to be published. These both deal with questions around prisons. During these years, Foucault was closely involved as the main sponsor of the so-called Groupe d'Information sur les Prisons (GIP – 'Prisons Information Group'), an organisation aimed at empowering prisoners to change their conditions by eliciting their testimony about their experiences. Clearly, the prisons were not only an activist cause for Foucault, but also the main matter of his theoretical reflection at the time, a reflection that culminated in his 1975 genealogy of the prison system, *Discipline and Punish*.

This book is extraordinarily close theoretically to *The Will to Knowledge* – unsurprisingly, given that the two books appeared in print within two years of one another. Questions raised in *Discipline and Punish* receive an extended treatment in *The Will to Knowledge*, perhaps most importantly the question of power. The lecture series extend the themes of both books still further. Foucault had begun to introduce his view of power by *Psychiatric Power*, his lectures of 1973–4. Here, he returns to the theme of his earliest works, the history of psychiatry, but now to a more recent period of it than that covered in his *History of Madness*, and applies his new genealogical method to it. The following lecture series, given in 1975 and entitled *Abnormal*, continues to deal with psychiatric themes alongside the theme of criminality (relating thus to *Discipline and Punish*) and sexuality (relating to *The Will to Knowledge*).

Abnormal thus shows the links between Foucault's long-standing research on madness, his newer interest in crime and punishment, and his work on sexuality, effectively tying together all his work of this time. The notion of 'abnormality', indicated by the title, is the key here: the mad and criminals are united in this category. As we will see, for

Foucault sexuality is also closely connected with questions of normality and abnormality. The sexual 'pervert' is a third type of abnormal person who has historically been linked by their abnormality with criminality and madness. This is not merely a conceptual association, moreover. The three categories have also been linked in institutional arrangements. The mad were for a long time – until the late twentieth century – generally incarcerated in asylums, and criminals continue to be incarcerated in prisons. Both these institutions only came into existence in their familiar form during the modern era, as Foucault details in the *History of Madness* and *Discipline and Punish*. The division between these two institutions decreased during the nineteenth century, as criminality came increasingly to be understood as a kind of mental defect. Sexuality does not have a specific institution of incarceration attached to it, but people have readily been labelled as mad or criminal or both on account of their sexuality and incarcerated accordingly.

A final course of lectures is also important for our purposes, *Society Must Be Defended*, which were given early in 1976, the year of the publication of *The Will to Knowledge*. These lectures give a genealogy of race and racism. Perhaps surprisingly, the theme of racism links very closely to what Foucault has to say about sexuality in *The Will to Knowledge*. The clearest point of overlap between the two works is the discussion what Foucault calls 'bio-power'. For him, sexuality and racism are prominent phenomena of this most modern form of power.

Later Work

After *The Will to Knowledge*, there followed a gap of over seven years before Foucault's next books, the final two volumes of *The History of Sexuality*, appeared in 1984. This is the longest gap between book publications on Foucault's CV. In the sixteen years between the publication of the *History of Madness* and that of *The Will to Knowledge*, he had produced books at a rate slightly higher than one every two years.

As one might expect, the books that appeared at the end of the hiatus showed great variation from what had gone before, notwithstanding that the books were notionally on the same theme as the previous one, sexuality. The first volume deals with modernity, the next two with ancient Greece and Rome.

At the time of the publication of *The Will to Knowledge*, Foucault promised readers 'at least six volumes' of *The History of Sexuality*,[15] with *The Will to Knowledge* to be followed by 'The Flesh and the Body', 'The Children's Crusade', 'Woman, Mother and Hysteric', 'Perverts' and 'Population and Races'.[16] These volumes all follow on from major themes of *The Will to Knowledge*; the first four of the five in this list correspond to what Foucault describes in this book as the four 'axes' along which sexuality developed. None of these eventuated, though two might correspond to lecture series that Foucault gave and which have now been published: 'Perverts' to *Abnormal* and 'Population and Races' to *Society Must Be Defended*.

They would have covered a historical span from the Middle Ages to the present. The final two volumes when they emerged were thus a major surprise to Foucault's readers, most of whom had in effect heard little from him during the intervening years, only those in Paris having had the chance to follow his lectures. Contrary to his original plans, he had found it necessary to trace the genealogy of sexuality back to the dawn of Western history, to ancient Greece. There was an intimation of this in the form of a footnote in the original *Will to Knowledge*, in which Foucault promised a study called 'Power and Truth' that would deal with questions of power in the ancient world, though this sentence has been excised in the translation (59/79). However, this is not what he delivered in the following volumes. The shift was not merely thematic, to the ancient period, but methodological. The second and third volumes of *The History of Sexuality* are relatively dry and historical, introduce comparatively few concepts, and are much longer than the first volume. Gone is the overt concern with power.

The rift between the first volume and the other two has been substantially filled in in recent years with the publication of the lecture series. The year following *The Will to Knowledge*, 1977, is the only year after Foucault's appointment to the Collège de France that he did not give a series of lectures there. It thus constitutes a something of a gap in the record of Foucault's thinking. After this, a change of direction is discernible. He moves away from an explicit concern with power, although he immediately remains greatly interested in political questions, which he explores now under the rubric of 'governmentality', a concept he himself coined and which has various meanings, which will be explored to some extent below. The main point of this concept I think is to allow himself now to reinsert the subject into his study of power. The general tendency of Foucault's last years is indeed towards the study of the subject, though this is a tendency that is already visible in the occasional posing of the question of the subject already in *Discipline and Punish* and *The Will to Knowledge*. This led him to questions more ethical than political. This is the essential difference between first volume of *The History of Sexuality* and the later ones: the first is about politics, the later two about ethics. That is not to say, however, that there is any incompatibility between the first volume and the second and third. Foucault's thesis in the final volumes is indeed complementary to his original thesis in *The Will to Knowledge*, although the two are not closely related. What we see from the final volumes is that the moral code of Western society has not changed much across history: broadly the same things are considered appropriate and inappropriate. What has changed is in how we relate to this code, which is to say how we relate to ourselves. This for Foucault is the domain of ethics, and of our self-relation more broadly. It is in this domain that sexuality can be said to arise: Foucault consistently thinks there is nothing like modern 'sexuality' to be found before the modern era.

Foucault's final publication schedule projected a fourth volume, *Confessions of the Flesh*, about sexuality in the Christian period between the late antiquity dealt with in Volume Two and the modernity previously dealt with in Volume One. This was in draft form only on Foucault's death, and seems unlikely ever to be published, leaving a link between the volumes missing. Some of Foucault's lectures of the 1980s, however, give glimpses into its likely contents, in particular his final, 1984 series, *The Courage of Truth*.

Notes

1. Foucault, *Archaeology of Knowledge*, p. 213.
2. Foucault, *Power/Knowledge*, p. 184.
3. Macey, *Michel Foucault*, p. 32.
4. Foucault, *Ethics*, pp. 163–73.
5. Quoted in Friedrich, 'France's Philosopher of Power'.
6. Macey, *The Lives of Michel Foucault*, p. 92.
7. Macey, *The Lives of Michel Foucault*, p. 30.
8. Eribon, *Michel Foucault*, p. 133.
9. Quoted in Friedrich, 'France's Philosopher of Power'.
10. Eribon, *Michel Foucault*, pp. 26–7.
11. Eribon, *Michel Foucault*, p. 29.
12. Macey, *The Lives of Michel Foucault*, pp. 86–7.

13. Macey, *The Lives of Michel Foucault*, p. 205.
14. Foucault, *Aesthetics, Method, and Epistemology*, p. 446/Foucault, *Dits et écrits* IV, p. 445.
15. Foucault, *Power/Knowledge*, p. 187.
16. Macey, *The Lives of Michel Foucault*, p. 354.

2. A Guide to the Text

Contesting the Repressive Hypothesis (Part One)

Part One, the shortest of the five 'parts' of Foucault's book, does broadly three different things: it both lays out and attacks what Foucault sees as a particular historical account of the history of sexuality, what he calls 'the repressive hypothesis', and also lays out the general stakes and content of the rest of the book. We will therefore deal with Part One under three subheadings: 'The Repressive Hypothesis', 'Critique of the Repressive Hypothesis' and 'Genealogy'. We round out the discussion of Part One with an additional section considering the repressive hypothesis, 'What Is the Repressive Hypothesis?'

Foucault does not draw clear lines between the different things he does in Part One. When describing the views he opposes at the beginning of Part One, he rarely notes that he is opposed to these views. That is, he for the most part simply expounds the repressive hypothesis as if it were his own view, before then starting to criticise it in turn, without marking the transition. Confusion is further compounded by the fact he uses the name of the view he is attacking, 'the repressive hypothesis', as the title for Part Two, in which he in fact puts forward his own views about what has happened, and not that hypothesis. Foucault has a reason for doing this: what he does in Part Two is to explain how the repressive hypothesis emerged, rather than what it is.

This all contributes to confusing readers as to the difference between the view he is attacking and his own views. In fact, as I will explain below, I think the indistinction is not only in readers' minds, but also in Foucault's own: he does not actually reject the repressive hypothesis in its entirety so much as make certain criticisms of it and to an extent build on it.

The title Foucault gives Part One refers to 'other Victorians'. He has taken this phrase from the work of Steven Marcus, who used it as the title of a study of the seedy underbelly of Victorian society (that is, Western society during the reign of Britain's Queen Victoria, the mid- to late nineteenth century). The 'other Victorians' were those who engaged in sexual activities that were officially entirely forbidden in Victorian society. The idea here is that, whereas Victorian society was generally puritanical and abjured sex, there was a dark side of this society in which wanton sex occurred, separated in certain districts of town, certain houses of ill repute, involving certain special people, the 'other Victorians'.

In the English translation, the title of Part One is 'We "Other Victorians"'. What does it mean then to say that *we* are 'other Victorians'? It implies two things at once. On the one hand, it could be taken to imply that we are like the other Victorians of Marcus's thesis: where the Victorians were prim and proper, we today are sexually brazen. On the other hand, it could imply that we are in fact just like the Victorians in prudishness, 'other' in the sense of being another set of Victorians later in time. Foucault's original French formulation is 'Nous autres, victoriens', which translates literally as 'We other ones, Victorians'. This is a pun on Marcus's 'other Victorians' (*autres victoriens* in French), that works by subtly inserting a comma in the middle of the phrase. Foucault's meaning here in fact is that we think ourselves to be very different to the Victorians, but actually we are much closer to them than we think.

The Repressive Hypothesis

As mentioned, he starts the book in Part One by outlining a view which he opposes, which he thinks is the conventional way of understanding the history of sexuality today. This view he calls 'the repressive hypothesis'. The repressive hypothesis claims that our recent history – the Victorian period to the present day – has been marked by an extraordinary repression of sexuality, which came into being with the imposition of a 'Victorian regime'. The period prior to this is seen within the repressive hypothesis as having been marked by a 'tolerant familiarity with the illicit' (3/9). This implies that sex in the pre-Victorian era was still illicit, proscribed, but discussion of it was not, only perhaps frowned upon as naughty. The Victorian regime is not then associated primarily with the banning of sexual acts themselves; after all, sexual acts of varying kinds outside of the marital bed had been considered sinful and had been illegal for centuries. The novelty of the Victorian attitude to sex then, according to the repressive hypothesis, was not that it banned sex itself, but that it tried to banish all overt signs of it. This banishment is not merely at the level of speech, but also display: according to the repressive hypothesis, the Victorians restricted not only the practice but the appearance of sex to the marriage bed (3/9). Sex is to be neither seen nor heard outside of that bedchamber.

Foucault does see the repressive hypothesis as allowing Steven Marcus's insights regarding 'other Victorians', that even in the midst of the Victorian regime there existed certain social spaces in which illicit sexuality was tolerated. Foucault refers specifically to two such spaces, what he calls the *maison close*, literally 'closed house', meaning a brothel, and the *maison de la santé*, a 'house of health' (4/11). He seems in the latter case to be referring in particular to psychiatric institutions, where people were confined, in many cases because of their sexuality. These then were both places where Victorians corralled illicit sex, as part of the more general programme of repression.

The repressive hypothesis, therefore, sees the Victorian regime as essentially confining sex: sex belongs within the marriage bed; where it overspills that, it is again confined in particular sites where it can be contained. Of course, such a confinement cannot be completely successful. Sex lurks everywhere, and this is why the regime is so repressive, because people have always to be on their guard for sex in order to repress it when it appears in the wrong place.

A perverse consequence of the confinement of sex is that sex becomes more or less compulsory in its limited sphere: one has to marry, and once married one has to have children, since sex is taken to be allowed only because of its reproductive function. If one does not marry, or marries and does not have children, it indicates one has not contained one's sexuality in the proper place; one is thereby taken to have shown a suspicious abnormality (3–4/10). This applies only to adults, of course: children, by contrast, since they are biologically incapable of reproduction, are taken to be abnormal if they show any sexuality at all. They are defined as sexless, and every sign of sexuality in them is repressed (4/10).

After the Victorian period, the repressive hypothesis sees the twentieth century as bringing with it the beginnings of a liberation. Sigmund Freud's invention of psychoanalysis at the end of the nineteenth century is credited with making a difference, since Freud insisted that we talk about sex precisely in order to deal with what he saw as the unhealthy repression of our libidinal urges. For Freud, ideas that are particularly unpalatable or difficult are hidden from our conscious awareness by a 'censor' that ensures that they are relegated to the recesses of our unconscious. This is what Freud calls 'repression'. According to Freud, such repression is ultimately ineffective, since the repressed ideas continue to exert pressure on the mind leading to neurosis.

It should be noted that the concept of repression invoked by Freud, which Foucault does not mention in his discussion in point of fact until much later in the book, is not quite the same as the notion of repression invoked in the 'repressive hypothesis'. In French, indeed, different words are used for each type of repression – *refoulement* for the psychological kind, with *répression* reserved for the social form – such that the distinction would be thoroughly obvious to readers of the original French.

The repressive hypothesis holds that our society is what is repressing our sexuality. This might involve psychic repression, but the repressive hypothesis sees the social repression as the primary problem. The repressive hypothesis thus disagrees with Freud: if there is psychic repression, it is caused by social repression, at least where sex is concerned. That said, Foucault does clearly think that Freud's theories lay the groundwork for the repressive hypothesis.

Freud allowed that Victorian attitudes did much to encourage psychic repressions, and made it impossible to cure them, from Freud's point of view, since for him the only cure was to talk about one's repressed feelings. From the point of view of the repressive hypothesis, however, this was inadequate. Psychoanalysis tries to deal with psychological repression without dealing with the social atmosphere that causes it. Freud only allowed people to talk about sex in the safe space of the psychoanalyst's office, in private between patient and analyst, and then only for the purpose of ensuring that patients behave themselves with more decorum outside that space, by dealing with their repression and learning to control, rather than simply repress, their libido. Individuals thus reconciled by psychoanalysis to the control of their urges will no longer pose a problem for the regime of sexual repression in society. For the repressive hypothesis, however, the problems the patients have are created by social repression in the first place, hence Freud appears to be perpetuating rather than curing the real problem.

However, Foucault notes, Freud could hardly be expected from the perspective of the repressive hypothesis to have overthrown the entirety of society's sexual repressiveness in one fell swoop. Rather, a revolution is required, one which involves not just speaking, but the breaking of laws and 'a whole new economy in the mechanism of power' (5/12).

Following in Freud's wake, the dissident psychoanalyst Wilhelm Reich formulated a position that a social revolution is needed to get rid of the social basis of repression, embracing Marxism alongside Freudian principles, before later developing his own very eccentric theories about energy and life. The repressive hypothesis would seem to be Marxist, in that it involves explaining cultural and political phenomena in terms of class and economic causes: it identifies the dawn of the Victorian regime with the dawn of capitalism, and correlates repression to changes in the mode of production (5/12). The specific link that Foucault thinks the repressive hypothesis posits between capitalism and sexual repression is that sex is repressed because it distracts the proletariat from their work (6/12). That is, capitalism was the first social system to be prominently concerned with the efficiency of its workers, and the extraction of maximum labour from workers might be taken to imply the elimination of all distractions, sex included. That does not mean that there was any attempt to completely eliminate sex, since sex is necessary to the repro-duction of the workforce, but that sex was to be kept to a minimum, with sex outside of the marital bed being judged only to cause problems in the workforce for the capitalist employers.

Here, Reich and the repressive hypothesis seem to be in agree-ment. Foucault does not identify Reich with the repressive hypothesis, however, at this point, though much later in the book he seems to acknowledge Reich's role as its originator (131/173). For now, Foucault indicates that the full repressive hypothesis bundles Reich with Freud as someone to be 'denounced', in Reich's case due to what Foucault calls Reich's underlying 'timidity' (5/12). It is not at all clear what this timidity resides in. 'Timid' is not the first word that comes to mind in relation to Reich's theories. Indeed, this timidity is far from 'obvious', as Hurley's translation has Foucault call it; the French in fact refers to a copious, rather than obvious, timidity (5/12*). We will return to this question of the repressive hypothesis's relation to Reich below under 'What Is the Repressive Hypothesis?'

Critique of the Repressive Hypothesis

Foucault does not explain himself, but rather begins instead to criti-cise the repressive hypothesis, noting that there is something suspi-cious about the way it posits political and economic causes, because it indicates that the repressive hypothesis requires some kind of 'serious' issue outside itself to link sex to in order to make itself seem important (6/13). This resembles an older phenomenon in which people had to excuse themselves before discussing sex by justifying why it is necessary to do so. This puts the repressive hypothesis in a self-contradictory position: it maintains that we should be unembarrassed about sex, but itself seems to need to justify talking about sex, to be embarrassed about according it importance.

The repressive hypothesis does not merely excuse itself for talking about sex, however: it insists on talking about it. These days, Foucault thinks, the repressive hypothesis has generated a general injunction on everyone to talk about sex, by casting sexual repression as a weighty political issue, and prescribing talking about sex as the solution. Any talk about sex has thus become a radical act of transgression, a political act in and of itself. Overcoming the embarrassment of talking about sex becomes something that proves our radicalism; to be embarrassed to talk about sex marks one out as a political reactionary.

Foucault claims that there is, moreover, a prophetic dimension to the repressive hypothesis that sanctifies it, in which the restoration of 'good sex' is promised (this is the phrase he uses in French, paraphrased in the translation – 7/14*). This type of prophecy is of course a feature of revolutionary discourses in general, as Foucault notes elsewhere.[1] The repressive hypothesis entails a prophecy of sexual revolution, just as Marxism entails a social one; indeed, from the point of view of the repressive hypothesis, these two revolutions would seem to be closely linked, if not simply synonymous.

The reference to 'good sex' is informative, because it implies that the stakes of the repressive hypothesis are not only discursive but sexual. That is, sexual liberation (a phrase that Foucault does not use, but that I will use to denote the end of repression that is the implied aim of the repressive hypothesis) is not only a matter of liberating speech, but of liberating sex itself. The implication is that our sexual repression is preventing us from enjoying sex. This may take the form either of the claim that our 'repressed' attitude to sex itself hampers our enjoyment, or that our lack of open talk about sex prevents us from learning practical things that might liberate our enjoyment.

There is such urgency then for people to talk about sex that they will pay for the privilege. In this way, sexuality (and not just sex itself, which people of course have long paid for) has become an industry. But it is also much more than that too. According to Foucault, truth, sex, liberation and the promise of the future have combined in an irresistible combination, such that it resembles a religion, its exponents preachers (7/15). It has, moreover, displaced the older revolutionary project, the difficult one by which people had to get together in a conscious organisation to change society (8/15). Now all that is required to make a revolution is to talk about and engage in sex.

Foucault thinks that this is manifestly not working the way it is supposed to. We have become (or had in 1976 at least, according to Foucault) a society that keeps telling itself it needs to open up and talk about sex and renounces sexual repressiveness, even though we are already talking about sex to an unprecedented extent (8/16). Foucault's point is that sexual liberation is not something new that threatens to shatter our society, but rather something that has been around for a long time and is not incompatible with the society it criticises. This point is similar to that he made in his book of the previous year, *Discipline and Punish*. That book is an examination of the prison system. It exposes the hypocrisy of incarceration by showing its historical stability. Specifically, prison has always promised to reduce crime, there have always been lots of people proposing prison reform, and people have always said prisons should rehabilitate prisoners, yet prisons have always produced recidivism (that is, that people who have gone to prison have always tended to commit more crimes on their release), and this effect has always been well known. As an overall effect, prisons produce rather than cure criminals, but while always operating with the excuse that prisons are not yet being run quite correctly, and that one day they will start to work. Something broadly similar is happening with sex: we are told we are repressed, and that we have to talk about sex, and that eventually we will be cured of our repression. But this is a pipe dream. What we find if we examine things objectively is that we are talking about sex a lot, while at the same time castigating ourselves for being repressed. Foucault indicates a continuity between the repressive hypothesis and earlier attitudes towards sex: where we once felt guilty about sex because it is sinful, we now feel guilty for having repressed it (9/17).

Foucault's critique of the repressive hypothesis coalesces into three specific, enumerated 'doubts' about the repressive hypothesis (10/18):

1. The 'properly historical question': is it factually true that sexual repression came into being in the Victorian era?

2. The 'historico-theoretical question': is power primarily to be understood theoretically as operating by repression?
3. The 'historico-political question': is the 'critical discourse that addresses itself to repression' actually opposed to a previous form of power or is it 'part of the same historical network as the thing it denounces'?

He immediately moves to dismiss a possible interpretation that, by raising these doubts, he means simply to answer 'no' to all of these questions and reject the repressive hypothesis completely, to claim there never was any great Victorian repression (10/19). He does not deny the repressive hypothesis outright in such a way. Rather, discussing the first of his questions, he is equivocal. He does not say there has been no repression, nor even that there has been less repression 'since the classical age' (12/20). 'The classical age', incidentally, had been part of the original subtitle of Foucault's earlier *History of Madness*; it is a phrase that has little currency in English, but in French refers to the great 'classical' blossoming of literature and culture in France in early modernity, particularly in the late seventeenth century, sometimes referring to a relatively short span of time, and sometimes to the entire period in English called 'early modern' (from roughly the end of the fifteenth century to the end of the eighteenth).

He is not denying that there has been a prohibition then, nor is he definitely affirming that there has been one. Rather, he wants to say that, even if it has existed, much too much emphasis has been placed on it in our account of the history of sexuality (12/21*). Ultimately, Foucault simply is not much concerned with this question of whether we are repressed. What interests him is all the talk about sex that has been produced on the pretext of combatting repression. Even if we wish to combat repression, it is not a priori true that this entails engaging in profuse discourse about sex. It is not necessarily true even that talking about sex tends to help us overcome any putative sexual repression: it is quite conceivable that we can talk about sex all day long and remain sexually repressed. The only repression we would seem to have overcome is a repression of sex talk – and Foucault is particularly dubious that this particular form of sexual repression ever existed.

Foucault does not think the repressive hypothesis is false then, so much as inadequate. He thinks it is definitely false only insofar as it poses as the single correct history of sexuality. It is not necessarily wholly false, however. Foucault sees the elements that the repressive hypothesis correctly identifies as operating in a much larger whole together with the repressive hypothesis itself. Rather than refute the repressive hypothesis outright then, he seeks to contextualise it, to understand our way of thinking about sex within a larger context than the stark historical framing provided by the repressive hypothesis. Just how this is possible will become clearer with Foucault's reconceptualisation of power later on in the book, but we can point already to his comment that the repressive hypothesis identifies a 'great central mechanism' (12/21): it sees there as being a single great apparatus repressing sex, whereas he complains that such identifications see things much too simply and ignore that great complexity of society.

It already is clear at this point that Foucault disagrees with the use of repression as a model of thinking about power in society in general. We commonly think of power as a negative force that prohibits, but Foucault's implicit claim at this point already is that power is in general *productive*, and its negative, prohibitive, repressive functioning is merely one part of its essentially productive operation. In the case of sexuality, the repression that we see is merely an aspect of something more interesting: the production of sexualities, of discourse about sexualities.

If we examine things in empirical terms, we find multiple tendencies in our society. We still encounter those who demand that sex be hidden and that it be discussed less. In particular, one may point here to the religious conservatives who still exist in every society today. Certainly, it was not the case in Foucault's day or today that literally everyone would agree with the repressive hypothesis: there are then as now many who think there is too much sexual libertinism. The repressive hypothesis is not supposed to be what everyone thinks, but rather how academics tend to imagine the history of sexuality. This is still a prominent view of the history of sexuality, however, and one that continues to find a practical correlate in those who decry repression and urge people to liberate their sexuality. The obvious way to understand this is to see two competing and opposing groups. But Foucault questions this logic. Although these groups may explicitly oppose one another, they are both components of a social whole.

When taken as a whole, our society is like the person who continually complains about their failings: as with such an individual, so with society we need to ask what function this self-condemnation serves. The repression–liberation combination has formed a relatively stable complex.

Foucault specifically looks at the discourse of sexual liberation, the repressive hypothesis, because it is here that the hypocrisy appears. Here are people who engage in a long-established litany of complaints against the contemporary establishment, aimed at revolution, without changing anything. We can ask about why people thought sex was sinful in the past, but today we need to ask why we feel guilty about such attitudes.

What Is the Repressive Hypothesis?

A couple of questions about the repressive hypothesis I think remain, insufficiently elucidated by Foucault. The first is the question of what Foucault means by calling it a 'hypothesis'. This word is generally used to describe an explanation that has some evidence in its favour but remains unproven, and hence does not have the status of a full-blown theory (literally it is what is 'hypo' – less than – a thesis). This is odd, since Foucault seems to posit the repressive hypothesis as a form of received wisdom, something that people definitely believe is right. One reason why he applies the word 'hypothesis' to it is perhaps that he thinks it is wrong, hence does not deserve to be called a theory. This does not ring true as an explanation, however, since ordinarily one would refer to one's opponents' position as a theory, and say that their theory is wrong. I think the ultimate explanation can only be that it is Foucault's own hypothesis, which he then seeks to explore, and indeed decides is wrong. That does not necessarily mean that it is Foucault's original invention (although I will discuss this possibility below). Rather, it implies simply that Foucault takes as a hypothesis for the purposes of his inquiry what others take simply as historical fact. Foucault is testing the established theory, and in doing so it is adopted as a hypothesis and tested in relation to the facts – and for him it is found wanting.

The second question relates to the big puzzle in Part One, namely how it is that from the perspective of the repressive hypothesis, Reich seems 'timid'. This, the big question here then, is whose views it is that the repressive hypothesis actually represents. Reich seems an obvious candidate, but is forcefully dissociated here. Without being able to identify anyone who actually believes in the repressive hypothesis, it would seem Foucault is simply setting up a straw person to attack. He speaks of the repressive hypothesis as if it were simply what everybody thought, at least in the West. However, as I have noted, I do not think that everyone, or even a majority of people, have ever held this view of the history of sexuality. Indeed, the repressive hypothesis as Foucault puts it forward for our consideration seems extraordinarily stringent. I will proceed by considering three candidates for actual representatives of the repressive hypothesis: (1) Herbert Marcuse and his followers; (2) Gilles Deleuze and Félix Guattari; (3) Foucault himself.

Marcuse and Freudo-Marxism

Marcuse is exemplary of the combination of psychoanalysis and Marxism in German thought in the early twentieth century to produce so-called 'Freudo-Marxism'. The most relevant text here is his *Eros and Civilization*, which Foucault references in *Abnormal*. Foucault indeed refers to Marcuse elsewhere in his corpus, indicating that he is familiar enough with his work to have got the idea of the repressive hypothesis from Marcuse. Foucault does not directly mention Marcuse in *The Will to Knowledge*, however, although he does use what seems to be Marcusian vocabulary in Part Four, as we will see below.

Marcuse does reject Reich, but in the opposite direction to the direction from which the repressive hypothesis apparently rejects Reich. Marcuse's problem with Reich is that Reich sees sexuality as a historically undifferentiated constant requiring liberation, where Marcuse sees sexuality as requiring a kind of careful handling.[2] Marcuse thus seems to be more, not less, timid than Reich, which is to say closer to Freud's position than Reich. Thus Marcuse cannot represent the full-blown repressive hypothesis.

I should, however, also mention a book that Foucault sees as slavishly following Marcuse, yet which Foucault refers to twice in *Abnormal* as doing what he is trying to avoid.[3] This is Jos Van Ussel's 1968 *Geschiedenis van het seksuele problem* ('History of the sexual problem'). It was translated into French as *Histoire de la répression sexuelle* ('History of sexual repression'), appearing in 1972, though it has never been translated into English. One could even suggest that this book's French title is whence Foucault derives the phrase 'repressive hypothesis'. Van Ussel has next to nothing to say about Reich, other than noting the latter's opposition to the repression of children's sexual instincts. However, while Foucault makes it clear that he rejects Van Ussel's approach because it focuses on an analysis of repression, this does not imply that it represents what Foucault will specifically designate as 'the repressive hypothesis' later in *The Will to Knowledge*. From Foucault's perspective all Freudo-Marxism, up to and including Reich, repeats the basic errors of the repressive hypothesis, but is not the full-blown version.

Deleuze and Guattari

Deleuze and Guattari's 1972 collaboration *Anti-Oedipus* dismisses Freud along with Freudo-Marxism and Reich, the latter two precisely because they are Freudian, which is to say, too timid. In relation to Reich and Marcuse they represent a hyperbolisation of the repressive hypothesis: where both Reich and Marcuse maintain that some psychic repression occurs necessarily, regardless of the social system (with the difference between them that Reich sees much more scope for getting rid of repression through revolution than Marcuse does), for Deleuze and Guattari all repression, psychic or social, is historically contingent and eliminable.[4]

There are several reasons why *Anti-Oedipus* is not a good match for the repressive hypothesis, however. For one thing, Foucault was extraordinarily close to Deleuze at this time, hence it would have been surprising for Foucault to attack the book. Indeed, he wrote laudatory preface to the English edition of *Anti-Oedipus* in 1976, the same year that *The Will to Knowledge* appeared.[5] That said, this does not prove that he did not disagree with the book seriously. His preface is clearly an exposition of Deleuze and Guattari's views rather than his own. Moreover, the fact there is no explicit mention of *Anti-Oedipus* in *The Will to Knowledge* would be the tactful way for him to both subtly oppose their position while maintaining friendly relations. As we will see below, on one point, the question of desire, he clearly disagreed with Deleuze. It is indeed odd that there is no mention of *Anti-Oedipus* or Deleuze at all in *The Will to Knowledge*, given how close the two men were, and how close *Anti-Oedipus* is to Foucault's thesis, in both time and content.

The closeness of their theses constitutes a second reason why *Anti-Oedipus* is not a good match for the repressive hypothesis. Specifically, *Anti-Oedipus* in its very title stands opposed to the valorisation of sex and the family in psychoanalytic thought, a position that Foucault largely recapitulates. There is no notion of 'sexual liberation' as such in *Anti-Oedipus*, no overt promise to make sex good again. One could argue that such agenda lurks in the background, but then the same thing could be said also of Foucault's book, as we will see. Still, there is a key difference between Foucault and Deleuze here in that Deleuze and Guattari explicitly view sex as repressive, whereas Foucault is trying to get away from repression as a notion.

A third reason that *Anti-Oedipus* does not fit the bill is that it does not give anything like the straightforward historical account that Foucault attributes to the repressive hypothesis in *The Will to Knowledge*.

Foucault's Hypothesis?

Indeed, the repressive hypothesis matches nothing so much as Foucault's own style. This leads me to my final contention, namely that the repressive hypothesis is essentially Foucault's own invention, not just as a straw person for him to argue against, but his own, genuinely held, but formative position.

According to Foucault's long-time life-partner, Daniel Defert, Foucault employed a kind of dialectical method in writing his books. He would begin writing a book by producing a manuscript expressing his initial view on the topic, which he would then deliberately set himself against. He would then conduct years of research, before rewriting the book. He would finally type a third version, cleaning up his thesis. Earlier versions he would deliberately destroy, leaving only the final manuscript.[6] In short, I think the repressive hypothesis is what Foucault thought about sexuality when he began to work on it, that is, the position of his initial manuscript.

Indeed, the repressive hypothesis resembles the position Foucault seems to have in his earlier work, in particular in the *History of Madness*. That book was not about sexuality, but it treats its subject matter, madness, as something that has been repressed. Foucault himself admits that the *History of Madness* employed the negative conception of power that he in *The Will to Knowledge* identifies with the repressive hypothesis and rejects.[7] However, he thinks that this conception was adequate to the historical period the *History of Madness* covered, which was earlier than that covered by *The Will to Knowledge*, even if the first book was in the final analysis not entirely satisfactory.[8] The earlier book in effect ends when the later one begins, such that the *History of Madness* deals with a historical period where negative forms of power were dominant. One can compare here *Psychiatric Power*, a lecture series in which Foucault takes up the themes of the *History of Madness* where he had left off chronologically in that earlier book, with the method of genealogy. Both *Psychiatric Power* and *The Will to Knowledge* according to Foucault deal with a period in which 'the technology of madness changed from negative to positive, from being binary to being complex and multiform'.[9] *Psychiatric Power* is made up of lectures given two years before the publication of *The Will to Knowledge*, but Defert gives three years as the typical gap between the first version of a book and the second in Foucault's production schedule. By the time of *Psychiatric Power*, Foucault had already repudiated the repressive hypothesis.

The repressive hypothesis then was Foucault's view in perhaps 1973 or earlier. It was doubtless conditioned by the ideas of *Anti-Oedipus*, his contact with Deleuze at that time being so close he scarcely could have avoided absorbing them, and indeed by his reading of Freudo-Marxist literature.

The fact that the repressive hypothesis had been Foucault's view goes a long way to explaining the vigour of his presentation of it at the beginning of the book, why he presents the repressive hypothesis primarily in his own voice and so convincingly, rarely noting that what he is describing is a view he will oppose. Of course, this presentation is intended to be ironic, but its lucidity reflects that Foucault has believed and indeed substantially continues to agree with the repressive hypothesis.

Genealogy

Foucault's disagreement with the repressive hypothesis is not a disagreement as we conventionally think of it, though it is a disagreement for all that. Ordinarily, disagreement is thought of as a disagreement over facts. Two opposing views are thought of as holding different things to be true, a matter typically then imagined to require reference to reality and experience to settle the matter.

This is, I think, a naïve view of disagreement in general, and it is certainly not how Foucault's rejection of the repressive hypothesis works. His reasons for rejecting it become clearer as one goes through the book, but some things can be said here at the outset. Foucault does not think that the repressive hypothesis is wrong about the facts. The facts it points to are accurate, for the most part. Most of the things it says happened did happen. Foucault disagrees with it rather as an interpretation of the facts.

Foucault produces his own study of the recent history of sexuality in Parts Two and Three. His own methodology here, genealogy, is based on facts, just as the repressive hypothesis is. This is a matter of picking out 'certain historical facts' that contradict the repressive hypothesis (13/22). This is a matter of pointing out facts that the repressive hypothesis ignores. But that is not to say that Foucault thinks he has now arrived at a complete and exhaustive account of all the facts, producing a final, accurate account of sexuality. The idea that history is capable of being so definitive is, I think, naïve. History is always selective: in order to construct a narrative, a story (the words 'story' and 'history' share an etymology, and in French there is only one word for both, *histoire*, as is the case in most European languages), evidence must be assembled and put together in a particular way. No history book simply lists facts, since this would produce an enormous, muddled and unreadable result (even a book of statistical tables must decide which statistics to present, and in what order). The difference between Foucault's approach and that of most historians is that he is quite open about his selectivity. This is the method of genealogy as history he lays out in his 'Nietzsche, Genealogy, History'. As he states in the very first line, genealogy is 'meticulous and patiently documentary',[10] but at the same time follows Nietzsche's notion of *wirkliche Historie*, 'effective history' as Foucault translates it, which lacks the pretence of traditional historical study, instead being openly tendentious. Foucault is quite conscious that he is on a collision course with academic historians.[11]

Selectivity is not the only thing that differentiates genealogy from the traditional form of history. Genealogy is also a form of analysis of 'discourses', as all of Foucault's mature work is. Foucault in *The Will to Knowledge* is analysing discourses about sexuality of the previous two centuries (though of course not everything said about sexuality during that time period, which would be an impossibly large task), up to and including the repressive hypothesis itself. This is part of what it means to do the genealogy of the repressive hypothesis, to understand where it has come from. By doing this, he undercuts it. The repressive hypothesis could be cast as a genealogy of repression, but Foucault trumps this by doing its genealogy. He can do the genealogy of the repressive hypothesis because he comes after it and is capable therefore of looking behind and beyond it. This might seem unfair, but this is simply an effect of the historicity of knowledge, that any knowledge, as soon as it has been articulated, is vulnerable to criticism that could not have existed without the thing it criticises.

The question Foucault poses of the repressive hypothesis is, as he puts it, that of its 'will to knowledge' (12/20): what drives this desire to know about sex, to talk about sex? However, in order for Foucault to describe and criticise the production of a discourse, he must himself produce a discourse to do this. This is not a discourse that stands outside of discourse, but a discourse much like any other, which in turn has its own will to knowledge. Foucault's will to knowledge is political. Genealogy is for Foucault a matter of doing what he in *Discipline and Punish* calls a 'history of the present'.[12] That is, 'genealogy' means a genealogy of the present, an account of where the discourses and forms of power we encounter today come from, motivated by a drive to criticise and subvert them, in order to change society. This means going beyond the liminal study of discourse, which preoccupied Foucault in some of his earlier work, to study its relation to other things. In this case, he sets out his intention to examine 'the links between these discourses, these effects of power, and the pleasures that were invested by them'.

We have three dimensions here then: discourse, power and pleasures. It will become clear by the end of our study here what he means by these words. At this point, 'power' and 'pleasures' remain relatively mysterious, since they are relatively new concepts in his work. 'Discourse', however, would be clear enough to anyone who had read Foucault's earlier works, and hence he does not spend much time here explaining what discourse is. Let us say for our purposes that 'discourse' is a particular way of talking about things, reflecting a particular 'knowledge', that is, a particular way of understanding the world, which cannot be disentangled from the discourse, the more concrete way of talking about the world. As Foucault says, 'it is in discourse that power and knowledge come to be joined' (100/133*). For him then, the task at hand at the end of Part One 'is a matter of determining, in its functioning and in its *raisons d'être*, the regime of power-knowledge-pleasure that sustains the discourse on human sexuality we have' (11/19*).[13]

Note the combinatory concept 'power-knowledge-pleasure'. Of the three concepts combined here, the first two, power and knowledge, are conventionally joined by Foucault in the hybrid concept 'power-knowledge' (see the Glossary below). 'Power-knowledge' could be described as the key concept of his genealogical method, the idea that power and knowledge are combined, such that any knowledge is linked at its very core to a form of power that drives it, and indeed vice versa. Why though does Foucault on this page, alone indeed in his entire corpus, amalgamate power-knowledge with pleasure? The full stakes of Foucault's invocation of 'pleasure' will be explored in the section on 'Bodies and Pleasures' below. What is implied here is that, firstly, pleasure is part of what has happened in the historical interplay of power and knowledge around sex. Sexuality is not only a matter of what we do (power), nor what we know, but of how we feel, where we get our enjoyment. Secondly, this usage implies that pleasure is for Foucault a key, categorical concept on a par with power or knowledge.

Foucault begins then with the discourses around sexuality, which means in the first instance the repressive hypothesis, what is being said about sex in his own immediate, radical milieu. He then seeks to understand this by linking it up to power and pleasure. The repressive hypothesis has its own account of its relation to power and pleasure: people say it because it is true, because they are repressed (by power), and because they desire freedom from repression so that they can enjoy sexual pleasure. Foucault's history of sexuality constitutes his refutation of that account.

The Explosion of Discourse (Part Two)

In Part Two, Foucault lays out his alternative to the repressive hypothesis, dealing with sexuality in the eighteenth and nineteenth centuries. He divides this into two chapters, the first relating to discourse about sex, the second to power in relation to sex.

Chapter 1: The Incitement to Discourse

Foucault begins Part Two, Chapter 1 with a paragraph restating the repressive hypothesis. He then contrasts this with an 'explosion' of discourse about sex that occurred during the last three centuries (17/25).

He next turns his attention to the question of the restriction of speech. He is characteristically cautious in his pronouncements: he suggests it is *possible* that a whole vocabulary was 'expurgated' (17/25–6).[14] Still, he acknowledges that some words at least were definitely banned (17–18/26). He endorses with near certainty the claim that there was a new economy of language that formed during the 'classical age', in which teachers and pupils spontaneously restricted their speech about sex, and masters and servants deliberately restricted theirs in relation to a new social configuration (18/26).

However, while certain direct expressions about sex were indeed repressed, the *amount* of discourse, indeed the number of distinct discourses, about sex increased continuously. Ever more is said about sex, in ever more ways. Some of this was perhaps an increase in people talking about sex in secret, but Foucault refers here only to the official talk about sex, since he can only study what has been written down (18/26–7). Such silences as there are, he goes on to claim, must be understood as part of 'strategies', which involve silences as well as utterances (27/38–9).

Foucault makes the point that silence always accompanies discourse. For all the things we say there must, by contrast, be things we do not say.

We cannot either talk all the time or say everything there is to say. There is nothing peculiarly suspicious or repressive about silence, then – it is in itself trivial, and inevitable. The question is what we are silent about at any given time, the reverse of the question of what we talk about at any given time (27/38–9).

Foucault gives an example here, an example which is the cornerstone of his entire account: the evolution of the practice of Catholic confession, by which believers confess their sins to priests, following the Council of Trent in the sixteenth century. Previously, priests had directly questioned penitents about the exact details of their sexual exploits. This explicitness was now suppressed. However, the frequency of confession was increased, and far more minor sexual details were asked for at confession, every thought, every indication of temptation to carnality (18–19/27). So, while it was less graphic, confession became much further reaching and more commonplace. This for Foucault sets the pattern for sexual discourse from this point on.

Foucault says here 'Mais la langue peut bien se châtier', a sentence hanging by itself at the beginning of a paragraph in the original French. It has a double meaning in French: it means either that language can be punished or that it can be polished. Indeed, both have happened here: language has been attacked in order to produce a more refined form of language. Something is taken away in order to enhance things. It is not clear who might ultimately be responsible for this, or indeed if anyone is: since the verb in French is reflexive, it could be taken to mean literally that language does this to itself.[15] Hurley's translation, 'language may have been refined', is taken by Dan Beer as an example of the problems of Hurley's translation and of translating Foucault (19/27).[16]

Proximally, of course, it is the Church and its clergy who are responsible. Their intention is now to arrest sexual desire long before it reaches expression in action, hence the sex acts themselves are no longer considered to be what is important: it is the intention, whether or not accompanied by action, that is now at stake. The very domain of the sexual itself thus undergoes massive expansion, from acts to ideas, thoughts and feelings.

An objection may be raised here that Foucault is locating a massive shift in Western culture in the Catholic Church, despite the fact that by this time much of Northern Europe had broken from the Catholic Church, even if Christianity in one form or another continued to dominate Western culture absolutely. The Council of Trent to which

Foucault refers had been called in part to deal with the question of the heretical Protestant churches that had split away from Catholicism earlier in the century. Within Protestantism, the status of confession varies, some churches practising it, others not, but none of them implementing the reforms of the Council of Trent.

Foucault is often Franco-centric in his remarks, despite claiming a wider applicability for his genealogies in Europe outside France. His focus on Catholicism in *The Will to Knowledge* is I think an example of this, France having consistently been a majority Catholic country. He does explicitly deal with the Protestant case, however, even if he does give more attention to Catholicism.

Protestantism and Catholicism have a shared history up to the Reformation in the early sixteenth century, when Protestants broke away from the Roman Church. Foucault goes on to detail some of this history in Part Three. Here, he identifies the origin of religious confession with the Lateran Council in 1215, centuries before the split. Foucault indicates, however, that there is a technological split occasioned both by Protestantism and the Council of Trent (116/153).[17] The identification of the divide as technological means that Protestants and Catholics from this point on use different techniques. While Protestants lack the formalisation of confession found in Catholicism after the Council of Trent, Foucault suggests that there may nevertheless be a 'certain parallelism' of Catholic and Protestant examination of conscience subsequently. That is, the two might mirror each other even where theological doctrine and techniques diverge. Particularly interesting in this regard is his remark in *Abnormal* that English Puritans engaged in a practice of 'permanent autobiography in which each individual recounts his own life to himself and to others, to those close to him and the people of his own community, in order to detect the signs of divine·election within this life'.[18] It is worth noting that Protestantism in fact was originally concerned to correct Catholic Christianity by paying more attention to intentions than to actions, and that Catholicism itself then substantially followed this tendency. The commonality between the two thus was not at the level of the confession as a sacrament, but at the level of the much more general imperative for people to 'turn their desire . . . into discourse' (21/30*). Rather than desiring sex, having sex, Europeans of whatever sect were encouraged to talk about sex.

At this point in his narrative, Foucault makes a surprising leap, from the seventeenth-century confessional to pornographic literature of the nineteenth century (21/30). The point of this leap is of course to join together two apparently highly dissimilar things, Christianity and pornography. Foucault's implication is that the commandment to transform desire into language of the Christian confessional is also the imperative followed by writers such as the Marquis de Sade, a French aristocrat whose notorious eighteenth- and early nineteenth-century literary descriptions of orgiastic sex and torture give us the word 'sadism'.

There is an ambiguity in such literature: are these reports of sexual engagements, discourses that reflect or accompany acts in real life, or discourses that substitute for acts? Foucault explicitly notes that the anonymous English author of the much later, Victorian work *My Secret Life* accompanies his life of sexual libertinism with an account of his doings.[19] However, given that this account is anonymous, it might have been entirely invented, or be entirely true, or any point in between. Sade's work is at least partly fictitious, though based in fact. In any case, the words may be supposed not merely to accompany life in the form of reportage, but as something that is in itself erotically enjoyable regardless of its relation to fact. Foucault points out that in the narrative itself, the editing of the piece is juxtaposed with eroticism – that is, that writing itself is an erotic exercise. Here too, a comparison is drawn with the Christian pastoral, in that one is in a sense supposed to enjoy the transformation of sex into discourse there too (23/32). Foucault's point is that what is common, from the modification of the confessional on, is the increase in discourse, and the correlation of this increase in discourse to some modification of desire itself and to the pursuit of pleasure. Our desire for and enjoyment of sex is thus displaced by a desire for and enjoyment of the act of confessing.

Still, there are self-evidently major differences between Catholic confessional manuals and *120 Days of Sodom*. The injunction to talk about sex has migrated out of the religious context. Foucault says that numerous 'mechanisms' were involved in this migration (23/33). Firstly, he names the 'public interest' (23/33). That is, sexual matters were held to be of public importance, and thus information about them was needed, for which purpose people had to talk about sex, not merely for the good of their souls, but in a practical and secular connection. This effort was hesitant for a long time: rational thought did not want to speak of something as base as sex (24/34). However, it had to deal with it, as a necessity of the administration of what was coming to be called 'population' (25/35). The link here is simple enough: governments were taking an interest in how many people were in their territory, and how healthy they were. This implied an interest in sex, firstly as the means of reproduction, and also as a means of transmission of disease. Sex was thus 'at the heart of this . . . problem of population' (25/36). Foucault will go on to expand on this topic at the beginning of Part Five; we deal with this below under the heading of 'Biopower'.

The point of taking an interest in the population was of course to attempt to shape and control it. It began with criticism of fruitless debauchery, which needed to be stopped, based on a belief that population increase was imperative. It developed into a more nuanced approach, marked by a belief that the rate of increase needed to be modulated differentially according to specific circumstances. This meant there was a need to encourage and teach individuals to 'control' their own sex (26/36). The state gathered information about sex to the end of formulating policies to influence people's sexual behaviour. Thus, there was a profusion of discourses about sex, both a discourse about it within the corridors of power, and discourses aimed by agents of the state at ordinary people.

Frank talk about sex with or in front of children is now restricted, but there was no shortage of people talking about sex in relation to children, and indeed talking to children about sex in a certain way was considered urgently necessary. Children now came to be seen as delicate developmental entities, who needed protection from certain realities (knowledge of which might turn them into prematurely sexual beings), and careful education to shape their sexual behaviour as adults in the right ways. This entailed an enormous, unprecedented concern with the sexuality of children: in this sense, children are paradoxically more sexualised than ever. One element of this was the pedagogy of sex, 'sex education' as it is called today, in which, as early as 1776, the facts of sex are taught to children in objective, scientific terms, supposedly without any embarrassment (29/40–1).

But this concern with sex is not restricted to children nor to verbal instruction. Foucault explores the example of the way educational institutions were architecturally designed around sexual concerns, for example (27–8/39). We have now mentioned discourses concerning sex within pedagogy, literature, religion, architecture and governmental administration. To this list, Foucault goes on to add medicine, in particular psychiatry, and jurisprudence. In doing so, he is mining the deep vein of research he has already conducted on these areas: his *History of Madness* and more recent lectures on *Psychiatric Power*, dealing with psychiatry; his history of institutional medicine, *The Birth of the Clinic*; his research on criminal justice, which had culminated in *Discipline and Punish*; and his lectures of the previous year, *Abnormal*, which had tied all these themes together. As can be understood from these texts, psychology and the prison system are closely related: modern punishment frequently makes use of medical categories. Where sex is concerned, a single category in effect unites medicine, psychiatry and the legal system: the category of *perversion*. Perversion was understood as a medically unhealthy condition, emanating from disease and having negative consequences for one's health, medical and physical. This notion thus added greatly to the perceived seriousness of sexual crimes: they were not just acts that contravened the law, but a public health hazard, something that needed to be nipped in the bud before it spread.

Here, Foucault gives an example that has come to be perhaps the most controversial in the book. It is controversial because it is a description of something that has in recent decades come to be seen as the most heinous behaviour imaginable: paedophilia. In the 1970s, in France, it is not clear that such things were considered quite so taboo. This shift in the seriousness with which paedophilia is regarded would seem to indicate the continuation of the tendency Foucault criticises – which is why his position is so controversial, because it seems to defend paedophilia.

He describes a case of a man, an itinerant labourer in rural France in 1867, whom Foucault describes as 'simple-minded', who had engaged in some kind of sexual activity with 'a little girl' (31/43). The man was reported, arrested, tried, sent for medical examination, and then despatched to spend the rest of his life in a mental asylum. What is important for Foucault about this case, it would seem, is that this was quite a new phenomenon. The acts of the man were nothing new to rural France, Foucault is at pains to state. It is rather both the criminalisation and medicalisation of his acts that were unprecedented. What Foucault really thinks is extraordinary here, as he states quite clearly, is the minute detail of the case, its 'minuscule character', *caractère minuscule* (31/44*). Hurley translates this as 'pettiness', which is not entirely inaccurate, but does not quite encapsulate what Foucault is getting at, and has perhaps contributed to the extent to which this passage seems shocking to contemporary readers. To say that the procedures were 'petty' implies that they were pointless and should not have taken place. Foucault, however, is merely noting how painstakingly the medical and juridical establishment dealt with such a commonplace act. The perpe-trator and victim were of no great significance, and such acts were surely not unusual – yet an entire book was written on this case, so much detail did the investigators go into. Similarly, Hurley puts the phrase 'incon-sequential bucolic pleasures' into the translation to describe the sexual abuse in question. This seems to imply that no consequences come from the sexual contact of a man with a little girl, that there is no necessary trauma from this. Foucault's words are *infimes délectations buissonnières*. *Infimes délectations* means 'tiny delights', but that does not imply they are inconsequential. *Buissonnières* is a difficult word to translate. Its usual con-notation is with truancy from school, but it literally refers to what is done in the bushes, which is presumably the location of the acts in question. I would suggest 'tiny delights in the bushes' as a more literal transla-tion. As long as the 'delight' in question is presumed to be that of the perpetrator, then this is unproblematic. Nothing in Foucault's account implies that he approves or disapproves either of the acts condemned as criminal or of the criminal procedure itself. He refers to 'timeless acts . . . between simple-minded adults and alert children' (31/44*), but the only claim here is that this kind of thing has always gone on, not that it is acceptable.

Today, I do not think it is an exaggeration to say that paedophilia has become one of a few paradigmatic moral evils that dominate our imaginary, alongside perhaps genocide and terrorism. In historical terms, what this case marks for Foucault is the point at which such acts passed from being given no great attention, to being a kind of public emergency. Doubtless it upsets people simply to be reminded that our absolutes are not absolute, that our sense today that adults treating chil-dren sexually is something uniquely and invariably horrendous is new to our society and not found anywhere else in history.

Foucault was critical of the taboo on paedophilia, of its absoluteness. He was involved in a movement in France, contemporaneous with *The Will to Knowledge*, to abolish age of consent laws entirely, effectively legal-ising all consensual sex between any persons, whatever their age. It is perhaps worth mentioning in this connection that in France paedophilia has historically been associated with homosexuality to a greater degree than in the English-speaking world. The term 'pederast' (a man who loves boys) has functioned in France as a synonym for a homosexual. This means that to campaign for gay rights in France brought one quite quickly into the domain of being concerned with the age of consent, not

merely in equalising it, but in getting rid of it. For whatever reason, for
Foucault, the concern about age and sex is of a piece with the modern
device of sexuality that he criticises and opposes.

This does not imply, however, that Foucault thought there was
nothing wrong with the historical abuse. In his fuller description of the
case in *Abnormal*, he notes that indeed consent was probably not given
here,[20] and he never advocated a legalisation of rape (though he does
propose considering it as common assault – we will look at this in much
more detail below).

For Foucault, what has happened here is part of a general tendency
for sex to be 'driven out of hiding' (33/45). Far from being covered up
in the nineteenth century, in a host of ways, sex was dragged into the
daylight of 'demography, biology, medicine, psychiatry, psychology,
ethics, pedagogy, and political criticism', from a previous existence as
a neglected and largely ignored facet of human life, only attended to
by the Church (33/46). This has not been an easy process, however: it
has led to 'tensions' and 'conflicts' (34/47). For Foucault, the conventional understanding, with the repressive hypothesis, of such tensions
is that there is a resistance of the status quo to the liberation of sex.
Foucault rejects this explanation, however: 'the secret of sex is doubtless not the fundamental reality in relation to which all the incitements
to speak about it are situated' (35/48*). Note that Hurley's translation
has Foucault say that the secret of sex is not 'in' the basic reality, which
unfortunately makes Foucault seem to imply that there is a fundamental
reality in relation to which all incitements to speak are situated, but that
the secret of sex is not part of it. Foucault himself says only that the secret
of sex is not a fundamental reality, and nothing about the existence of
any fundamental reality or of a relation to it in discourse more generally
here.

The core point in any case is that the secret of sex is not like DNA,
some hidden but important fundamental real thing to be discovered.[21]
The incitements to speak are thus neither attempts to smash (*briser*)
nor latch onto (*reconduire*) some reality behind sex. Rather, the secret
of sex is 'an indispensable fable' in the proliferation of discourse about
sex (35/49*), a mythical reference point by which all this explosion of
discourse is justified. It is held that if we keep speaking, we will discover
the secret bedrock of sex, but the secret of sex maintains its permanent
mystery, hence providing an inexhaustible aim for discourse. What our
Western late modernity has invented is not the secrecy of sex, which

was always there, insofar as there were always some prohibitions on speaking about sex, but the idea that this secrecy must be ended through an infinite elaboration in discourse that uncovers its true nature. This elaboration can never end the secrecy, however, since there is no real kernel there to be discovered. We imagine that the secrecy surrounding sex has guarded some treasure that can be reached through speaking and dispelling the secrecy, but this treasure does not exist.

Chapter 2: The Perverse Implantation

Foucault begins the second chapter of Part Two by considering a 'possible objection' to what he has said so far (36/50). This is basically Marxist in complexion, and demands that the explosion of discourse posited by Foucault in the previous chapter be analysed in terms of economics and class. This objection would argue that the explosion of discourses about sexuality is allied to the reproductive needs of capitalism as an economic necessity.[22] The objection attempts to recuperate the logic of the repressive hypothesis, by seeing the increase in discourse as essentially repressive, trying to restrict sexuality to its useful reproductive function, eliminating perversion.

It is on this last point that Foucault disagrees with the objection. As we have seen, he does think that there is at least one new discourse about sex that is partly economic in motivation, that is concerned with population. But, for him, what occurs here is not a restriction, but a massive proliferation of not only discourse but of sexuality itself (37/51).

Having clarified this point, he resumes his history of sexuality, adding more detail. He first looks at how things were immediately before the proliferation of discourse. At this time, before the end of the eighteenth century, there were 'three great explicit codes' governing sex: 'canon law, the Christian pastoral, and civil law' (37/51*). The first of these is a law within the Church, the second the advice the Church gave to believers, and the last the ordinary law. All of these codes' treatment of sex, Foucault says, centred on marriage, on telling people what they could and should do within marriage. All sex outside marriage tended to be grouped together, homosexuality with adultery, and not given much attention, beyond being banned. There were distinctions between more and less odious forbidden acts, of course, but it was only within the marital context that fine-grained distinctions of appropriateness were made. The 'law of nature' was invoked here in extreme cases of forbidden acts, with hermaphrodites (people of indeterminate sex) being

themselves in a sense illegal, but for Foucault there was no special attention to this category (38/53).

The 'discursive explosion' changed this by shifting the focus out-
wards. The codes did not initially change. What changed was the focus:
the married couple tended more to be left more alone, attention instead
moving to the '"unnatural"' (38–9/53–4).

On this point, Foucault spends a page or so discussing the famous
story of Don Juan (39–40/54–5). This story has many versions, often
using the Italian version of his name, Don Giovanni. It first appeared
in the sixteenth century, and has been reiterated ever since. The major
motif is simply a male protagonist who has seduced a great many women,
but eventually gets his comeuppance. The implication here seems to be
that Don Juan's conquests, while heterosexual and so not in themselves
in the unnatural order, are so extensive that Don Juan himself entered
into the order of the unnatural in his desires, and hence needs to be
punished. Foucault's point here is important if subtle, namely that what
is unnatural ceased to be a matter simply of acts, but something that
applied to persons in themselves: what Don Juan does is natural, but he
is personally taken to be unnatural. This explains Foucault's sarcastic
sentence at the end of the paragraph on Don Juan directed at psychoanalysis and its categorisations of persons (40/55). What has appeared is
a new category of person, the unnatural person, the *pervert*.

Perverts were subjected to a variety of classifications (40/55–6). They
were medicalised, which is to say that they were treated as sick. The
repression of people who engaged in unnatural acts lessened insofar as
they were less likely to be punished as criminals, but control and surveil-
lance were extended (40–1/56). This extension included everyone in its
purview. To hunt out abnormality, everyone had to be examined, since
it was not known in advance where abnormality lurked. This meant
that, although there was less attention paid to the 'natural' marital
couple, married couples also fell under suspicion of being unnatural,
and so were anything but immune from this trend. Medicine 'forcefully
entered the pleasures of the couple' (41/56*).

So there is an increase in control over sex. However, for Foucault the
change has not only been of how much sex is controlled, he thinks, but
of the very nature of that control. Different things are now allowed and
prohibited, by different means.

Firstly, Foucault thinks that more recent forms of control over sex
have a peculiarly paradoxical nature, indicated already in his remarks

about the 'secret of sex': he claims that the very thing supposed to be prevented, be it perversion or sexuality itself, is constituted in the very measures purportedly directed against it. That is, where earlier forms of prohibition of sexual behaviour tried simply to stop banned forms of behaviour where they appeared, the more modern form of control interferes to produce sexuality in order to control it, even if it does not present itself in this way, but rather presents itself as being like older forms of intervention, as combatting something that exists independently of it (42/58).

Secondly, as we have seen, rather than merely categorising acts as earlier laws had, the new form of control categorises individuals themselves according to their acts, that is, as various types of 'pervert' in accordance with their behaviour. As an example, Foucault here notes that this is how, in 1870, the modern notion of a 'homosexual' emerged, that is, of someone who has a definable sexuality in the sense of what is today called a sexual 'orientation'. Homosexuality is understood now not as a punishable act someone has done, as the older notion of 'sodomy' had implied, but as a matter of someone's very nature, who they are. This took the form of a positing of a 'hermaphrodism of the soul', which is to say, the belief that, though externally of one sex, in their depths such people were of the other sex, such that homosexual men were taken to be internally feminine (43/59). Their every action is understood in light of this classification. Everything the homosexual man does is understood to be discernibly 'gay', as we say today, and his sexuality to be obvious from his most mundane acts. It is not even required for the homosexual to actually engage in same-sex sexual congress to be so identified any more.

Foucault sums the situation up by declaring that 'The homosexual is now a species' (43/59*). In the nineteenth century, they are a species alongside many others. Foucault lists these many types 'entomologised' (that is, turned into an entomology, literally the study of insects) by nineteenth century psychiatry.

He lists first Charles Lasègue's 'exhibitionists' and Alfred Binet's 'fetishists' (43/60*). Oddly, Hurley simply drops these two Frenchmen from the translation of the list, though perhaps this owes to the fact that these two species are not particularly exotic, in that the terms are in circulation in common parlance today: an exhibitionist is one who shows off their body, typically naked, and a fetishist is one whose sexual desires focus on peculiar objects or 'fetishes'. Things get more exotic then with two German-speakers' categories which Hurley does include: Richard von 'Krafft-Ebing's zoophiles and zooerasts' ('zoophile' is still in circulation as a description of one who is sexually attracted to animals; 'zooerasty' is no longer used as a term, and referred to more extreme cases of people who were attracted *solely* to non-human animals) and Hermann 'Rohleder's auto-monosexualists' (a 'monosexualist' is someone with a sole sexual interest – that they were auto-monosexualists implied that they were interested in sex only with themselves, that is, in masturbation; 43/60). Both Rohleder's classification and his prescribed cure for it, circumcision, have fallen out of favour since. Then comes a little list of perverts with no authors attached: 'mixo-scopophiles [people who enjoy watching others having sex, i.e. voyeurs], gynecomasts [men who develop breasts – a kind of physiological perversion, then], presbyophiles [those who wanted sex with old men, a form of what these days is called gerontophilia], sexoesthetic inverts [Havelock Ellis's term for transvestites], and dyspareunist women [women who feel pain during sex]' (43/60). Some of these categories were actually invented in the early twentieth century, rather than in the nineteenth as Foucault suggests, though doubtless he is right to locate this profusion of categories primarily in the nineteenth century.

Beer argues that in lists like this, Foucault 'parades' psychiatrists and their categories as in 'a freak show', thus that Foucault's prose here is 'parodic'.[23] That is, where the psychiatrists of the time were creating a freak show with their categorisation of sexual perversions, with the perverts as the freaks, Foucault now turns the psychiatrists and the categories themselves into a freak show, easily making them look bizarre and ridiculous. This effect is accentuated by the fact that he does not (as I have done above as a supplement to him) explain who any of these psychiatrists are or what their categories mean.

Ridiculous though they may seem to us now in many cases, these categories produced a reality, as can be seen in the example of homosexuality in particular. Homosexuality seems entirely real to us today. When we speak of 'sexuality' today, this seems even primarily to apply to the question of whether one is homo-, hetero- or bi-sexual. Foucault thus speaks of a 'permanent reality': categories are implanted 'into bodies' as well as accreting in conduct (44/60*). We move our bodies, shape them, change them on the basis of a sexual identification. But homosexuality started out as just one of a menagerie of possible categories, most of which would not seem to have survived. This would seem to indicate a certain contingency in the notions we do have – one could perhaps imagine a world in which a different perversion came to be popularly applied in place of homosexuality, though there are doubtless reasons why homosexuality is the category that has come to occupy this place, even if Foucault does not investigate this question. Certainly, the level of prominence that homosexuality and the homosexual/heterosexual distinction have in the modern world is not found in other historical cultures. Thus, the reality of sexuality is produced rather than something we are 'just born with'.

Thus, even when homosexuals were persecuted, the mechanisms of power that identified people as homosexual were producing their homosexuality at the same time as they were persecuting people for being so identified: 'The mechanism of power that pursues this whole disparate collection only pretends to suppress it, while giving it a visible and permanent analytical reality' (44/60*). My translation here diverges significantly from Hurley's translation: he says that power here 'does not aim to suppress'. This might be true of power itself, that the mechanism of power itself as such does not aim to do this. Those who created these categories, however, did aim to suppress homosexuality – it is simply that the categorisation in practice constituted the patients in a way that tended to cement their perversions, and suppressed nothing.

A third difference in the current form of control of sex compared with previous forms is its much greater 'proximity'. We are now observed more closely, and experience more regular interventions to get us to speak, where previously power would wait for gross indecencies to occur, and act against them where they were publicly visible or reported. Power no longer waits but anticipates. It achieves a direct contact with the body and becomes entangled with our experiences of pleasure in ways that will be explained. Foucault presents the exercise of power here as pleasurable on both sides: the doctors enjoy examining the patients, and the patients enjoy being examined, producing '*perpetual spirals of pleasure and power*' (45/62; original emphasis). Thereby, 'power anchors the pleasure that it came to dig out of hiding' (45/61*). Hurley's translation errs here in the same direction as he does elsewhere: he has Foucault saying that power has 'uncovered' pleasure, when Foucault's point is that it intended to do something of that nature but did not.

Fourthly, there are what Foucault calls the '*devices of sexual saturation* so characteristic of the space and the social rituals of the nineteenth century' (45/62; original emphasis). What does this odd phrase 'devices of sexual saturation' mean? The sexual saturation is the extraordinary attention paid to sex during this period, and the devices are effectively the institutions through and in which this happens: schools, the family, etc. This is a distinct point to the point about proximity, because it refers not to the closeness of control, but to its extension and profuse complexity. Far from being a simple society based around the family, the family was striated and spatially organised in a way that it previously had not been, for example with the introduction of rooms of varied functions and individual rooms allocated to individual persons in ordinary people's housing. Categorised perversions are one aspect of this new complexification and spatial organisation. Perversity, Foucault asserts, is at the core of our society, not merely a function of sexual repressiveness (47/65).

For Foucault, the profusion of perversions produced 'multiple sexualities' well beyond the contraction of all the exotic categories of perversion previously listed (47/65*). We now have sexualities indexed to our age (infantile or mature sexuality, teenage sexuality), indexed to our 'tastes or practices' (such as homosexuality), ones indexed to our 'relationships' (for example as patient or doctor), and ones indexed to space (in the home, in the workplace, etc.) (47/65). These correlate to particular 'procedures of power' which 'solidify' the sexualities (47–8/65): 'The growth of perversions . . . is a real product of the interference of a type of power on bodies and their pleasures' (48/65–6*).

How it is possible for power to produce perversions will become clearer once we read what Foucault has to say about the nature of power below. For now though, we can understand his point that there is nothing about power that is opposed to pleasure. Foucault argues here that the proliferation of sexuality is neither essentially repressive nor deliberately planned. People accede to the categories, enjoy them. The fact that a myriad of commercial interests are invested in producing these sexual pleasures does not make the pleasure less real, for example. Indeed, the whole thing works precisely because the pleasure is really pleasurable. This is Foucault's final answer then to the imagined Marxist objection raised at the beginning of the chapter: far from being austere, capitalism here operates perfectly well through the production of diverse pleasures. Even if capitalism has to repress people at some point to operate, it can harness mechanisms that are in no sense repressive. Our society is one of a great decentralisation of power, of a sophistication of power, of unprecedented linkages of power to pleasure, not one of monolithic repression (49/67).

The Confessional Science (Part Three)

Psychiatry, Psychoanalysis and the Secret of Sex

Foucault begins Part Three by imagining another partial objection in defence of the repressive hypothesis (53/71). Again, it is allowed that there has been a tremendous profusion of discourse. This time, the objection defends the idea that the discourse has buried the secret of sex, rather than really paying attention to it – at least until Freud. This objection is not Marxist like the previous one then, but psychoanalytic-oriented. It claims that prior to Freud, investigations of sex were pseudo-scientific, subject to moral qualms around talking about the nasty details of sex. This pseudo-science set itself up as the guardian of public hygiene, via pseudo-Darwinist eugenicist and racist programmes (54/73). Even though science in the nineteenth century knew about sex via biology, it shrank back from thinking it through when it came to humans: biology acknowledged the reality of sex, while medical science refused to (54/73). Foucault characterises the distinction here as between a will to knowledge on the one hand and a 'will to nonknowledge' on the other (55/74).

Foucault accepts that the science of the nineteenth century did have all these failings with respect to sex, but resists the distinction between forms of will. Rather, he thinks that 'not wanting to recognise is another adventure of the will to truth' (55/74*). This is a Nietzschean point: all knowledge emanates from the will; it is always partial. Moreover, as Foucault has already noted, silences are as much a necessary part of a particular discourse as the things that are said within it. He also includes 'misunderstanding' as something that always involves 'a fundamental relation to truth' (55/74). The word Foucault uses here, which Hurley translates as 'misunderstanding', is *méconnaissance*, literally 'mis-knowledge'. This is a word that lacks an entirely adequate translation into English. For this reason Hurley takes the unusual step of retaining the French word in brackets on the next page, p. 56. Elsewhere Foucault explains the relationship of *méconnaissance* to truth more straightforwardly, saying 'la connaissance est toujours une méconnaissance': 'knowledge is always a misknowledge'.[24]

He refers here to the example of 'Charcot's Salpêtrière'; that is, to the work of Jean-Martin Charcot at the Salpêtrière hospital in Paris. Charcot is considered the father of modern neurology. He was well known for his public demonstrations, which were attended by, among others, a young Sigmund Freud, who himself trained originally as a neurologist. The Penguin edition of Foucault's book with 'WILL TO KNOWLEDGE' on the cover shows a painting of one of Charcot's public displays underneath the book title. These displays are what interests Foucault here. Charcot incited sexual displays from patients, 'hysterical' women, with the help of a 'sex-baton' (presumably in effect a dildo) and amyl nitrate (today best known as a party drug) (56fn./75fn.). While this extraordinarily salacious display was allowed, Foucault points to the fact that, at a crucial moment, when the woman was too aroused, things were stopped and the woman was removed, and the more lurid details of what was shown were excised from reports.

One thing that this shows is how psychiatrists produced sexuality, here in a literal, visceral sense. The restraint at the limit shows us something more than that, namely that they are producing the secret of sex. Once again the English translation loses the complexity of what Foucault is saying. Hurley gives us 'they constructed around and apropos of sex an immense apparatus for producing truth, even if this truth was to be masked at the last moment'. But what Foucault says is simply that the apparatus was constructed to produce truth and to stop and mask it at the last minute (56/76*). The difference is that Hurley's translation implies, in a way that Foucault does not, that there is a kind of tension between masking truth and producing it, and that the masking is a kind of inessential extra. But Foucault's very point here is that the constitution of a zone of silence is in no way opposed to the construction of truth, and that this specific apparatus was supposed to produce truth and mask something, both as essential, connected aspects of its operation. That is, the truth that is produced requires a hidden secret of sex.

Foucault's most basic point here is that sex is a matter of truth, not just of pleasure (57/76). But the specific truth here is one that includes masking sex: that is, the truth of sex for the nineteenth century included the idea that sex needed to be concealed to some extent. The Charcot example might seem to indicate that there is a secret that nineteenth-century medicine fails to penetrate. Foucault's point, however, is that this is not a failure but rather deliberate. The secret of sex is constituted as a secret, and as such is not to be penetrated, even while the science of sex appears to be aiming to expose it. The truth of sex is what is being demonstrated by Charcot, but this includes the principle that there is something of sex that cannot be demonstrated, that there is a secret of sex. In this respect, psychoanalysis for Foucault does not break with the psychiatric knowledge of sex of the nineteenth century, because psychoanalysis also posits a dark secret of sex, one designated by the name of Oedipus, which stands for incestuous desire: the secret we hide, even from ourselves, according to Freud, is that we wanted to have sex with our parents. This, for Freud, is an unpalatable truth that we can never fully accept or live with, hence that must remain essentially hidden. The repressive hypothesis is by contrast credited with claiming that there is nothing that must remain hidden.

Ars erotica and *scientia sexualis*

Foucault then shifts register dramatically, leaving the critique of psychoanalysis to one side for the moment, towards a world historical account of the relationship between sex and truth. He now leaps back in history much further than he had at any earlier point in his career, and broadens the geographical scope massively, again in a way unprecedented in his writing, declaring that there have been 'two great procedures for producing the truth of sex' in history (57/76). In the ancient Western world and in the Orient, the procedure followed was what Foucault calls, using a Latin phrase, *ars erotica* – erotic art. This procedure begins with erotic pleasure, and draws truth from that, through practical experience, through learning how to use this pleasure. Sex is thus not subjected to absolute rules, but is a question of pleasure-intensifying technique, involving learnt, practical knowledge, which can be taught by experts. There are secrets here too, things that are not divulged because their secrecy increases the pleasure. These are not like the later 'secret of sex', however: these secrets can actually be learnt, though presumably the promise of 'absolute mastery' and eternal life held out in relation to them is illusory (58/77).

That said, Foucault actually later withdraws the characterisation of ancient Western sexual practices as an *ars erotica*, after investigating these practices for the second and third volumes of *The History of Sexuality*:

One of the numerous points where I was wrong in [*The Will to Knowledge*] was what I said about this *ars erotica*. . . . The Greeks and Romans did not have any *ars erotica* to be compared with the Chinese *ars erotica* (or at least it was not something very important in their culture). They had a *tekhne tou biou* in which the economy of pleasure played a very large role. In this 'art of life,' the notion of exercising a perfect mastery over oneself soon became the main issue. And the Christian hermeneutics of the self constituted a new elaboration of this *tekhne*.[25]

Tekhne tou biou translates as the 'art of life', but 'art' in the broad sense of a 'technique' that encompasses both aesthetic and practical concerns.

The distinction between an art of life and an erotic art is somewhat subtle, and indeed Foucault indicates here that the two are not mutually exclusive. The major difference is the lack of emphasis among the ancient Greeks and Romans on sex or pleasure, which they subordinated to more general principles of self-mastery.

One could also question, though Foucault himself does not here, the applicability of the notion of *ars erotica* to Eastern societies, moreover. The idea of Oriental societies as worlds of sensual pleasure is an old European exotic fantasy, and does not seem to correspond to contemporary Asian culture, though perhaps it once was true of the society that produced the Kama Sutra.

Such questions are relatively unimportant for our purposes, however, since *The Will to Knowledge* is about the kind of procedure that, according to Foucault, we have uniquely adopted in Western modernity, what he calls *scientia sexualis* – sexual knowledge. *Scientia* in Latin means 'knowledge' in general, rather than what we would today narrowly call 'science', though it certainly includes that, and we certainly do have a sexual science today, as Foucault goes on to explain.

What is unique about the modern West's sexual life is not that we have knowledge about sex, however.[26] In some sense, presumably all cultures have that. Foucault, talking about the book after its publication, coins the term 'over-knowledge' (*sur-savoir*) to describe the *scientia sexualis*. It is rather then that we have much more knowledge than we need, that we overproduce and overconsume knowledge about sex. This of course is what Foucault has been saying about our relation to sex from Part One onwards.

Foucault does allow that an *ars erotica* has survived in our society. It survives to the extent to which we have, through Christianity to the modern day, engaged in rituals that do produce pleasures. This technical production of pleasure exists though only subsumed under the *scientia sexualis* as a special pleasure derived from our search for knowledge about sex (71/95). It is not the healthy sex that our procedures purport to aim at that grants us pleasure, but the process of seeking the secret of sex via confession and treatment. Foucault sits on the fence here regarding the question of whether our *scientia sexualis* is a form of *ars erotica* or vice versa (71/96).

History of Confession

The centre of our *scientia sexualis* is confession. Foucault now gives a fuller historical account of confession than he has previously in the book. Confession gained prominence in Western societies in the Middle Ages, he tells us. One form of this was in the Church, as already detailed, but it also gained prominence as a procedure in jurisprudence: criminal justice moved from a system of tests of character (swearing oaths, physical trials, testimonials) towards the detailed confession as the primary determinant of truth, with all the ancillary interrogatory practices that entails (58/77). It did not entirely replace the older tests, but confession took pride of place amongst them (59/78).

Since then, Foucault thinks, confession has got everywhere – into our personal relationships, for example (59/79). One is supposed to confess to one's partner, children are supposed to confess to their parents, and even parents to their children. Literature now frequently takes the form of a confession (59/79–80). Foucault points out that, historically, the 'shadow' of confession has been torture, used to force out the confession where it is not given voluntarily (59/79). One hopes that this has at least partly ceased to be the case in our era of human rights where torture has been banned (even if there if it continues in flagrant violation of these norms in many cases). But if the instance of torture has declined, this can be taken to demonstrate only that the confessing impulse has become so ingrained that torture has ceased to be necessary. Foucault's claim indeed is that the procedure of confession has become so habitual that we think of it as natural, and not as the operation of power (59/80). For him, the repressive hypothesis is indicative of this, in that it presents power as what prevents an entirely natural confession from spilling freely out of us. What we see from looking at the historical case of confession is that this is not so, that telling the truth is encouraged by and conditioned by power (60/81). Foucault holds that at the moment people were first brought into this confessing culture, it must have seemed an onerous imposition, but over time this perception has diminished.

This historical impulse to confess is for Foucault related to deeper changes in the constitution of our very selves wrought by power, which are necessary to make us perceive confession as natural. He discusses these changes first in terms of 'individualisation' (59/78*): he thinks we are 'individualised', made into individuals by these procedures. This very notion that individuality is produced runs contrary to the dominant idea in our society that we are naturally individuals and that expressing our individuality is the highest form of freedom. For Foucault, however, the categories by which we construct our individuality are on the contrary a recent imposition. This operates via what we might call our 'identity', a phrase Foucault uses in a couple of places in this book, though not very prominently (e.g. 156/205). We confess to an individual identity, which, contrary to our impression, does not exist independently of our self-identification, but is constituted by the confession itself.

The second term Foucault uses here, which is related to, though not exactly the same as that of 'individual', is 'subject'. Foucault speaks here of our 'constitution as "subjects" in both senses of the word', a process he calls 'subjection' (*assujettissement*) (60/81*). The two senses of the word 'subject' are, on the one hand, being subject *to* power, in the sense of being subject to the law, and, on the other hand, being the subject *of* action, the grammatical subject, the one who does things.[27] That is, we are constituted as both passive and active subjects through the process of confession. Foucault's invocation of subjectivity here is interesting for showing that he was interested in the question of the subject well before it became a more prominent theme in his thought in the 1980s.

Confession makes someone into a subject in these two senses in a very direct way: she is the subject of confession both in the sense that she is the one who makes the confession, and in that she is the thing that the confession is about (61/82). The truth of the confession is guaranteed simply by the absolute proximity between the one who speaks and what they are speaking about (62/84). It is true that confession is only effective when it is heard by someone else (61/83). This person who hears confession, the confessor, potentially has a very active role in the confession, laying down its rules, and its consequences (61/83). However, they are not supposed to have the knowledge – their ignorance is in a sense their qualification. They are trying to find out about us, moreover. In our society we are subjected to power by being encouraged to constitute ourselves as subjects, to understand ourselves as autonomous actors, in relation to another, thereby giving ourselves up to them, creating ourselves in a way that makes us more comprehensible and therefore malleable. Implicated here is the historical movement, already dealt with earlier in the book, of confession from a concern with relatively superficial acts to our innermost intentions (63/85).

Foucault jumps here from dealing with the development of the Catholic confession to the case of a Serbian partisan during World War II (60–1/81), a kind of fast-forwarding through history almost to the present. Why this specific example? I take it that it is chosen for its relative obscurity. A 'Serbian partisan' implies two things: an Orthodox Christian by culture (rather than a Catholic Croat) and a communist. This indicates that confession has grown to encompass not only non-Catholic Christianity, but its opposite within Western culture, atheist Marxism. Confessions have a starring role in the history of Marxism-Leninism in the twentieth century, we might note, most obviously in the show trials of Stalin's Soviet Union, in which individuals were compelled to confess to sometimes preposterous charges. It was not enough for them to die, which was in many cases a foregone conclusion from the moment they were accused; they had to confess. This technique is found everywhere: here, an obscure nobody in the mountains, who has rejoined his comrades (presumably implying that he had previously deserted), must adequately account for himself and his wrongs through autobiography.

Sex is implicated in all this as a 'privileged theme of confession' from the Middle Ages to modernity. Conversely, confession is privileged from the point of view of sex, as the main connection between sex and truth in our society (61/82). Foucault now details the way the confession of sex came to have this importance, by spilling out of the religious ritual into other places, most obviously medicine, but also the family, the school and the prison (63/84). Confession itself had changed, and came now to be about 'bodies and life' rather than sin (64/86).

Foucault lists 'Campe, Salzmann, and especially Kaan, Krafft-Ebing, Tardieu, Molle, and Havelock Ellis' as responsible parties (63/85). Joachim Heinrich Campe was a German lexicographer who was also active in the campaign against children's masturbation in the late eighteenth century. Christian Gotthilf Salzmann was a German contemporary of Campe. Heinrich Kaan and Richard von Krafft-Ebing were both originally from Austria, and each wrote a separate work of nineteenth-century sexology bearing the same title, *Psychopathia Sexualis*. Auguste Ambroise Tardieu was a nineteenth-century French forensic medical scientist who wrote about the sexual abuse of children. Havelock Ellis was a late nineteenth-century British sexologist who later became a psychoanalyst. 'Molle', I have concluded, given the chronological order of the figures, is a misspelt reference to the nineteenth-century German sexologist Albert Moll.

These names then are united by being either the leading exponents of classical sexology (the science of sex) or its forerunners. Foucault only mentions sexology once in the book, in Part One (5/12), and names these men only as 'nineteenth-century psychiatrists', though the first two were active in the late eighteenth century, meaning that they preceded sexology per se. These men invented the science of sex in the strict sense. They did this, according to Foucault, by reassembling the confession of sex that was by then dispersed through various social institutions. There was a problem of incorporating confession into science, however: the scientist is used to trusting the evidence of his own senses, whereas using confession as a source of data meant becoming dependent largely on the confessions of others (64/86–7). Foucault indicates how the imperative to confess was made scientifically respectable:

1. Confession was clinically codified as a scientific procedure (65/87).
2. Sexuality was postulated as causally implicated in all kinds of disease, thus endowed with vital importance (65/87–8).
3. Sexuality was understood as latent, the truth of sex as difficult even for the subject of it to extract, therefore requiring guided confession (66/88–9).
4. The interpretation of confession was seen as requiring a qualified person, hence giving a role to the scientist (66–7/89).
5. Sexuality was classified as either normal or pathological, and confession was understood as therapy for pathology (67/90).

Thus, 'for almost one hundred and fifty years, a complex device has been in place for producing true discourses about sex' (68/91*). It is this device that has made 'something like "sexuality"' 'appear as the truth of sex and its pleasures' (68/91*). 'Sexuality' then is merely an effect, not what is discovered by sexology so much as the 'correlative of that slowly developed discursive practice that is the *scientia sexualis*' (68/91*). This does not mean that sexuality is an illusion for Foucault, however. It is, rather, something produced in reality. To have a science of sex, we need sexuality to really exist, and for Foucault it is the science of sex that brings it finally into existence. This sexuality is pleasurable, moreover, although sex simultaneously becomes a tenebrous secret, and becomes 'an object of great suspicion' and of 'fear' in the process (69/93).

Part Three ends with a three-page section, from pages 70 to 73 in the English version, that mainly repeats what has been said already, or prefigures what will be said later, about which section I will therefore say nothing specific.

The Analytic of Power (Part Four, Chapters 1–2)

Part Four begins with a prologue relating to Denis Diderot's eighteenth-century French novel, *Les Bijoux indiscrets* (*The Indiscreet Jewels*). The key device of this novel is that of a ruler, Mangogul, who has a magic ring that makes genitalia (the 'jewels' of the title) talk to him. This is intended as a satire on contemporary France, but it is its explicit content that concerns Foucault: after all, we have here a literal case of 'sex which talks', confession made flesh, as it were (77/101). It should be noted here that in French the word *sexe*, translated into English by its cognate 'sex', has a wider meaning than it does in English. In English, this word has two main meanings: it can mean sexual intercourse (coitus) or the biological sex of animals (male/female). In French it has, in addition to these two, a third meaning: it can refer to the genital organs. A vagina or a penis can hence be referred to as a 'sex' in French. It is in this sense that Foucault is here talking about 'sex'. It is worth bearing this connotation in mind whenever Foucault uses the word 'sex'.

Inserted in this prologue are further ruminations about sexuality in modernity. Here, Foucault deals with the relation of sex to reason. Sex we might expect to find understood as 'pure mechanics without reason' (78/102*). Rather, we find the opposite: it is not even that sex has just been 'annexed' by reason, but rather that sex has become the dominant logic by which everything about ourselves is understood (78/103). The prologue ends with some open questions: why is the truth of sex so difficult and so secret? Why was it so important?

Before answering these questions, Foucault sets the scene by spending two chapters discussing the nature of power in society. Although these chapters are supposed to help his genealogy along, they clearly greatly exceed this local mission. Foucault is following up the intention he announced at the very end of Part Three to 'study strategies of power' and 'constitute the "political economy" of a will to knowledge' (73/98). Foucault explains the notion of 'strategies of power' to some extent in what follows, though he does not revisit the notion of a 'political economy of a will to knowledge'. Political economy ordinarily refers to a simultaneous study of politics and economics, their interaction. However, Foucault's references to 'economy' in *The Will to Knowledge* are not usually to economics in the ordinary, English-language sense, but rather reflect a more general sense in which the French word *économie* is sometimes used, to refer to an arrangement of any stable structure;

hence, for example, his invocation of an 'economy of discourses' (11/19). 'Political economy' here I think then refers to the organisation of power itself, though this meaning is far from obvious, hence perhaps Foucault's use of scare quotes around the phrase.

The reconception of social power is possibly the most significant single contribution of Foucault's entire life's thought. The passages dealing with power in *The Will to Knowledge* are the mainstay of this reconception. In an interview about the book shortly after its publication, he claimed that the material on power was what was most essential to it.[28] It certainly seems to me that Foucault's account of power is the most important thing in it, because it is the most general in application: sexuality may be ubiquitous to our society, but power is even more significant to it, and of greater historical importance, moreover. What Foucault has to say about power is accordingly the densest and most confusing part of the book, and as such will require detailed explication.

For all its importance, the material on power arrives without fanfare. There is very little earlier in the book, and nothing in the book's table of contents, to indicate its presence. We have rather two chapters with unrevealing one-word titles. This is not exactly disingenuous of Foucault, however. Perhaps it would be better to describe him as modest here, because what he does in effect is couch the most original account of power ever as an incidental methodological tool for his inquiry into sexuality.

It would be wrong to suggest, however, that this material on power is merely developed for this study. Foucault started talking about power early in the 1970s. Reflections on power substantially similar to, but not as detailed as, those made in *The Will to Knowledge* are found in his book of the previous year, *Discipline and Punish*,[29] and his lectures of earlier the same year, *Society Must Be Defended*, contain parts of the account.[30] Still, *The Will to Knowledge* has the most polished version of Foucault's 1970s account of power; it is only really exceeded in an extension first published in 1982, 'The Subject and Power', about which I will say something once I have explored the relevant chapters from *The Will to Knowledge*.

In the first of these two chapters on power, Foucault critiques the conception of power we have today; in the second, he gives us his alternative conception.

Chapter 1

Chapter 1 is entitled *Enjeu*, which Hurley translates as 'Objective'. Strictly speaking, though, *enjeu* does not refer to the 'objective' of the study, but rather to its 'stakes', in the sense of 'what is at stake'. The objective of a game is not the thing that is at stake in a game. Power is not the objective of Foucault's study, but it is what is at stake in it. What this chapter is about is the conception of power that is in play today.

Psychoanalysis

Foucault starts Chapter 1 by acknowledging that psychoanalysis is more complicated than the repressive hypothesis. Psychoanalysis has up to this point in the book been neglected by Foucault, except for a single passing mention earlier on.

While it is clear from what has been said already that the repressive hypothesis develops out of psychoanalytical perspectives, he now points out that psychoanalysis in fact has a more sophisticated view of repression than that indicated in the repressive hypothesis.

I take it that the form of psychoanalysis Foucault primarily has in mind here is Lacanian, that propounded by the French psychoanalyst Jacques Lacan. This is what one would expect Foucault to have in mind, as Lacan was the pre-eminent psychoanalyst in France at the time, where his followers dominated not just psychoanalysis but the institutions of psychiatry and psychology, as they have continued to since. As Foucault does not name Lacan, however, this reference is not explicit. There is a certain indistinction in any case between Lacan and psychoanalysis more generally, because Lacan sees himself as fundamentally faithful to Freud and the psychoanalytical project, and other forms of psychoanalysis as having diverged from Freud.

The particular insight of psychoanalysis that Foucault now refers to is one that is fundamental to psychoanalysis or peculiar to Lacanian psychoanalysis, depending on your orientation. It is namely that, as Foucault puts it, 'it is the law that is constitutive of desire and of the lack which establishes it' (81/108*). This is Lacanian vocabulary: 'law', 'desire' and 'lack' are all key terms in Lacan's thought that are rarely found elsewhere in psychoanalysis. Certainly, for Lacan, it is what he calls 'the law' that allows us to determine our desire, though this does not mean the law in the strict sense of the rules enforced by the state, so much as the fundamental principles of a culture.

Foucault acknowledges such a position is similar to his inasmuch as it implies that power is always already at work in desire. Like Foucault then, psychoanalysts do not think of power and desire as opposing forces, by which the former simply represses the latter. Though psychoanalysis is foundational to the repressive hypothesis qua theory of repression, psychoanalysis itself does not think of sexuality as repressed in general and requiring liberation. It is indeed because of this that the repressive hypothesis dismisses psychoanalysis.

Repression and Law

Foucault accuses himself now of having failed to distinguish adequately in the earlier parts of the book between repression and law (82/108). He imagines others criticising his own position for failing to have dealt with the problem of law by simply bundling it with the problem of repression. He further imagines that he will be criticised even in relation to the problem of repression, for himself making use of a notion of power to criticise it, when power and repression are essentially the same thing, making his critique another repressive hypothesis. Some would indeed later criticise *The Will to Knowledge* on this basis.

Foucault's pre-emptive response is to defend bundling together repression and law, while distinguishing both of them from the concept of power. His does this by claiming that both the repressive hypothesis that takes repression to be diametrically opposed to desire and the psychoanalytic viewpoint that takes law to be constitutive of desire appeal to the same essentially negative conception of the operation of power. This conception of power is not exclusive to this domain of thinking about sex, but is rather generally held in our society. Foucault now lists the key features of this dominant Western conception of power:

1. Negativity: power is thought of as consisting in various kinds of negative relation, as being something that operates by saying 'no' to things: it refuses, denies, excludes, hides.
2. The rule: power is always thought of as involving laws or rules. Foucault repeatedly calls this conception of power 'juridical', which reflects the centrality of law to it. This means that power is about establishing '"order"' (though Foucault puts the word in scare quotes, perhaps because he thinks our conception of order is also problematic), while also providing 'a form of intelligibility', that is, providing the way for us to understand things. In the case of sex, it

is perceived as ordered by law/rules, and that conditions our under-standing of sex deeply, as allowed or forbidden.

3. Prohibition: this is, I think, what one gets from the combination of negativity and the rule: if power is negative, and it is rule based, then what it produces are essentially prohibitions, rules saying what you cannot do. This carries the implication that one will be *punished* for breaking the rules. Foucault indicates that there is a kind of double negativity to the traditional conception of power here: either the forbidden thing is negated, which is to say it does not happen, or the one who does it is negated. When it comes to sex, there is a reflexivity to power on this conception, in that the thing to be negated is under-stood to be part of ourselves, so the traditional account of sexual repression has us either negating ourselves (by denying our sex) or facing negation from without as the punishment for failing to negate ourselves.

4. Censorship: Foucault thinks that censorship is imagined to take three distinct forms – banning something altogether, preventing speech about a thing, and denying that it exists at all. He argues that all of these forms are seen as connected. We are banned from talking about something in the hope that if we do not talk about it, this thing will cease to exist in reality. Conversely, things which are not supposed to exist cannot be topics of conversation. Sex of certain kinds is not sup-posed to exist, is not allowed to be practised and cannot be discussed. However, Foucault's implication is that this is an inadequate view of censorship that takes it to be purely negative, though he does not elaborate on what a positive form of censorship might be at this point.

5. 'The unity of the device' (84/111*): power is supposed to be a single thing that is uniform throughout its structure, working the same way everywhere at all times, only differing in scale. The best example of this in traditional political thought is the idea that a king is like the father of a family, and indeed vice versa. Thus, the foregoing four features are supposed to be repeated at all levels. A hierarchical, top-down organisation across levels is assumed, moreover. The rela-tionship of monarch and subject is understood as key to the whole edifice, with political society being a series of master–slave relations stretching from the top down to the bottom (85/112).

Foucault notes further that power is traditionally conceived of as unin-ventive and simple, on either the model of repression or that of law

(85/112). It is seen as having no energy of its own, rather only operating to hold back that which does have energy.

For Foucault, this negative conception of power is so obviously inadequate to understand the profuse and sophisticated forms of power we find around us, that he thinks the predominance of this conception itself requires an explanation (86/113). The explanation he offers is that 'power is tolerable only on the condition it masks an important part of itself' (86/113*). That is, power in effect produces the traditional conception of power as a necessary mask to conceal its activities, since if we knew what it was really like, we would not accept it any more. In our society, we can accept power as a negative limit on our freedom, but if we knew that it was producing our behaviour, we would not stand for it.

Foucault might seem to be contradicting himself by saying now that power conceals itself, since one of his criticisms about the traditional conception of power is that it sees power as something that conceals. Moreover, it seems here that Foucault is presenting the truth as being inimical to power, whereas he famously says earlier in the book that truth is not automatically on the side of freedom (60/81). However, he does not claim that power does not conduct negative operations, nor that truth cannot challenge power, but rather only that it is inadequate to understand power as essentially negative or truth as essentially opposed to power. An example of a truth that does not challenge power would be to point to instances of repressive power in defining power: repression really does exist as part of power's operation, but this basic truth is acceptable; it is the truths that Foucault is now bringing to light that he thinks are not acceptable to power.

Foucault then gives a historical account of power and our conception of it to explain where our current ideas come from. He tentatively suggests that our traditional conception of power is medieval in its origins. In the Middle Ages, certain institutions of power, principally the monarchy and the state, grew to prominence. These were based on pre-existing 'powers', but also brought something new in opposition to what had come before (86/114). Their growth produced a complicated, tangled situation, but the new institutions found acceptance by presenting themselves as bringing order to chaos. They presented themselves as simple, and unitary, organised in a clear hierarchy. This involved a new construction of the law, to some extent based on the revival of older Roman law (87/115).

This then was the original point at which power masked itself with the conception that has lasted to this day (I do not think it has significantly declined since 1976 when Foucault was writing, despite his efforts to expose it). Even in the Middle Ages, there already was a considerable disjuncture between the way that power operated in practice and the way it was presented in theory. In theory, the king's authority was absolute, but in practice, he only ruled by complicated strategic deals with noblemen who could and did unseat rulers who were not to their liking. Moreover, the power of all such powerful men depended on a certain pliancy on the part of ordinary folk, whose refusal to obey, whose peasant rebellions, were a constant threat that had to be reckoned with. In the face of this potential and actual resistance to his rule, the monarch was able to increase his power by mobilising the law that referred to him (87/115). As Foucault points out, though, he would break this law when it suited him (88/116).

When someone wanted to overthrow a monarch, rather than oppose the entire edifice of law supporting the monarchy, the usurper would use the law. The monarch's violations of the law, for example, could provide a convenient excuse for someone seeking his throne. When the monarch was deposed then, it was in the name of a truer interpretation of the law, even if his replacement could in his turn be relied upon to play loose with the law in practice to some extent himself. The law as an institution is nevertheless strengthened through this process as a reference point for politics, and the conception of power itself as law is also strengthened. This then is the story of the bourgeois revolutions of the seventeenth and eighteenth centuries, in England, the USA and France: the old monarchical power is deposed in favour of a more stringent application of the rule of law in the republics that replace them.

In the nineteenth century, however, criticism of the law itself did emerge. This 'more radical' form of criticism did not condemn power for being inadequately lawful; rather it accused the law itself of being a disguised form of violence (88/116–17). However, thinks Foucault, that criticism still implies that we should change things to produce the exercise of power according to a *droit fondamental*, literally a 'fundamental right', which Hurley gives as 'fundamental lawfulness' (88/117). Foucault does not make clear either who specifically holds such a view, or what this fundamental *droit* might be, so it is hard to assess the veracity of his claims.

It seems obvious enough that the more radical critics in question must be people like Marx, socialists and anarchists in the nineteenth century who proposed not only to abolish monarchy, but to abolish the state and the legal system. While some such socialists and anarchists, particularly in the early nineteenth century, did refer to juridical or moral notions, this criticism seems misplaced when applied to Marx, who pointedly refused to have anything to do with such ideas. Socialism at its extreme in the nineteenth century seemed simply to oppose any form of power at all, any law or repression, at least in its final goal, while also refusing any moral foundation for this opposition. There is, perhaps, however, a lingering 'law' in the form of a 'law of history' that Marx still retains, which assures him that his cause is right, since the revolution he preaches is inevitable. It is certainly true in any case that such thinkers had a traditional conception of power; it is just that unlike earlier thinkers, these radicals dreamt of abolishing power altogether. Foucault's point, against them, is that abolishing old forms of power such as law and the state will not constitute the abolition of power as such.

Thus, Foucault is right to conclude that no one prior to himself had deposed the monarchical conception of power. Hence his famous conclusion: 'In political thought and analysis, we still have not cut off the head of the king' (88–9/117). This is a reference primarily to the guillotining of Louis XVI of France in 1793, following the French Revolution. Foucault is often misinterpreted here as meaning that politics has changed since the French Revolution and that our political thinking has not caught up with these changes. This is not his point, however. Politics has not changed fundamentally by Foucault's lights, and neither has our way of thinking about it: both are essentially as they were in the Middle Ages, even if there have been many relatively profound changes, which Foucault indeed details. The point is that the form of political thought we have was inadequate even before the eighteenth century and the decapitation of King Louis. The problem that Foucault refers to by telling us there has been a failure to cut the head off the king in political thought is that, even though with the Revolution people saw through the ruse of monarchic power, the fictitious aura of absolute authority around the king, they have not seen through the same aura around authority more generally; the conception of power that sustained the monarchy by masking its impotence remains in place.

Foucault claims that while the juridical model of power 'could be useful for representing' the older form of power, albeit imperfectly even in that case, it is utterly inadequate to representing the newer form

(89/117–18).The change in the form of power that does occur at this time from one based on 'deduction (*prélèvement*) and death' to one based on the control of living bodies (89/118) is dealt with by Foucault in the final part of his book.

The upshot in relation to sexuality is that we are still thinking about the relation of power to sex on the old, inadequate juridical model. This leads to the repressive hypothesis, by which we think that all power does is impose restrictions on our behaviour. Foucault proposes instead, 'in looking a bit more closely at all the historical material, to advance bit by bit towards an alternative conception of power' (91/120*).

Chapter 2

It does not seem to me, however, that this is the procedure he follows. What he does in the book is to move immediately on in Chapter 2 to expound a new conception of power without any fresh reference to evidence. Foucault indeed seems slightly disingenuous here. He suggests that his theoretical reflections here are thoroughly subordinate to his historical inquiries, and that they are only made tentatively as an aid to the latter, yet he proceeds to propound a view of power he has already developed elsewhere in distinct contexts, and which seems only partly to enter into a relation with the historical evidence he has given in relation to sexuality.

Foucault calls his account of power an 'analytic' (*analytique*) as opposed to a 'theory' (82/109*; 90/119*).[31] By this he signals his intention to analyse power, rather than define it. It also indicates that he considers his approach here still to be tentative, as opposed to being a finished theory. Still, this unassuming second chapter, simply entitled 'Method', contains what is perhaps his most decisive theoretical intervention. It is thus the densest and most important part of the book.

By itself, Foucault's focus on power sets him apart from traditional political thought, which was concerned with objects typical of the juridical conception, such as repression and law. An example of this, though Foucault was not at all familiar with it, would be recent political philosophy in the analytical tradition, which provides the orthodox political theory taught today in universities. This focuses on questions of 'justice', 'equality', 'freedom' and 'legitimacy' – all juridical concepts. There was some reflection on the nature of power in mid-twentieth-century American political philosophy, but Foucault would not have been aware of this and it does not noticeably inform contemporary political philosophy. It in any case corresponded to the conventional understanding of power that Foucault criticises.

Foucault does not here engage in anything like the history of political thought, however. He does more to couch his approach in historical terms at the beginning of *Society Must Be Defended*. Here, in *The Will to Knowledge*, he mentions only Machiavelli as a precursor to his own approach, and one who was inadequate, in that, living half a millennium ago as he did, he continued to refer his analysis of power to the person of the prince (97/128).

Foucault's Account of Power

Foucault is immediately careful to distinguish what he means by 'power' from '"Power" as a group of institutions'. He wants to make clear that he is not using 'power' in ways it has been used within the traditional conception of politics, for example as roughly synonymous with the state, or as synonymous with repression, with something negative and juridical that keeps people down (92/121). This is the sense of 'power' that we encounter in political slogans such as 'fight the power'.

One should note that the English word 'power' can have two translations in French, *pouvoir* or *puissance*. Foucault uses the word *pouvoir* here. Whereas *pouvoir* means 'power' in a legal or political sense, *puissance* means 'power' in a physical sense. Foucault says that *pouvoir* is not a *puissance* ('strength' in Hurley's English translation; 93/123). That is, Foucault is not talking about the kind of mechanical power that machines – or indeed humans – have.

Foucault launches into his reconceptualisation of power without warning in the first paragraph of Chapter 2. What he unleashes is a shock to the system. I am going to break what he says down idea by idea in order to explain it.

He starts by saying 'that power must be understood in the first instance as . . .' (92/121), followed by a long sentence in multiple clauses, broken into four parts, each of which is quite dense.

The first part of the sentence declares that power is 'the multiplicity of force relations which are immanent in the domain where they are exercised, and which are constitutive of their own organisation' (92/121–2*). This is only the first part of a much longer sentence, but there is a lot here already. Firstly, there is the notion of a 'force relation', for which Foucault provides no explanation. Why Foucault talks about power in terms of 'relations' becomes clearer as he goes on, but the notion of 'force' does not. In fact, in this book Foucault uses the phrase 'force relation' almost as much as the phrase 'power relation'. There is a similar pattern of usage of these phrases in *Discipline and Punish* and *Society Must Be Defended*. The word *force* in French has a slightly more general meaning than in English, implying strength in general, not just violence. I think the easiest way to deal with this word is simply to take 'force relation' and 'power relation' as synonymous. Doubtless, Foucault had some reason for choosing to use 'force' rather than 'power' here, but it is not clear what that is.

The notion of 'multiplicity' is not explained either. This word implies that a large number of distinct elements are combined together in a larger whole without any single unifying factor. This is already a departure from the conventional understanding of power, which sees it as unified around a central core.

To say that power relations are immanent means that they exist locally, in the specific context that they occur, rather than referring back to some great power or law outside of that situation. Foucault further holds that the power relations organise themselves, rather than relying on a coordinating agency, such as the state or the law.

The second part of the sentence describes power as 'the game which, by way of incessant struggles and confrontations, transforms, reinforces, and inverts them' (92/122*). Hurley here translates Foucault's 'game' (*jeu*) as 'process'. This is an odd translation, and misleading insofar as it makes the reader think that Foucault definitely describes power as a process (he does not do so, despite very frequently using the word 'process' [*processus*] elsewhere in the book). However, Hurley does get Foucault right inasmuch as 'process' implies that for Foucault power is perpetually changing. Foucault's point in this passage is that power is a game, not in the sense of having final winners and losers and points, or indeed in the sense of having rules, but in the sense that the outcome is not fixed in advance, that things go back and forth and are contested endlessly. This notion of the game becomes more prominent in Foucault's later accounts of power, after *The Will to Knowledge*.

The third part of the sentence has power as 'the support which these force relations find in one another, so as to form a chain or a system, or, on the contrary, the differences and contradictions which isolate them from one another' (92/122*). Power is here understood as encompassing both the mutuality of force relations, which work with one another, and also the way in which they fail to cohere with and contradict one another. The idea is introduced here that power produces structures, and that this occurs through the interaction of power relations, without any central direction.

The last point of the sentence is that there are 'strategies in which they take effect, and whose general design or institutional crystallisation is embodied in state apparatuses, in the formulation of the law, and in social hegemonies' (92–3/122*). Here, Foucault introduces the idea that the regular structures of power are 'strategies'. For him, these include the kinds of things referred to in the traditional conception of power, such as the state and law. These are not rejected by Foucault's conception of power so much as now incorporated into a greatly expanded conception.

This long sentence then gives way to a flood of exposition of his conception of power. Foucault insists next that our investigation of power should not be governed by the search for a central point, something implied by multiple things said in the first sentence. He asserts that the operation of power is rather a matter of a 'moving base of force relations, which, through their inequality, incessantly engender states of power, but ones which are always local and unstable' (93/122*). Power is in some sense portrayed here as basic, underlying the visible effects. The production of the relatively stable politics we see is an effect of the very instability of this base. That is, power is a matter of contending forces that through their jostling with one another come to a kind of inherently unstable equilibrium, producing the surface effect of apparent order, under which they continue to jostle, this jostling itself holding up the surface edifice. Power is for Foucault 'everywhere'; not because it is a single thing that takes everything in its grip, but rather because 'it comes from everywhere', as incessant, local, ubiquitous force relations that underlie everything (93/122). The solidity of power is an appearance only, one that is produced as the 'overall effect' of all the contesting relations. The English word 'concatenation', used here in the translation, very precisely describes the effect Foucault means to identify with the rather vaguer French term *enchainement* ('linking').

Foucault then proclaims his 'nominalism', that is, his belief that 'power' is ultimately just a name applied somewhat arbitrarily to a more elusive reality. Power is not then an entity in its own right that has an undeniable, cohesive, objective existence, but rather 'the name we attribute to a complex strategic situation in a given society' (93/123*).

His idea that power is really a matter of contending forces and his use of the word 'strategy' both relate to his suggestion here that we should understand politics on the model of war. He does this, famously, through the deliberate inversion of a famous saying of the German general and military theorist Carl von Clausewitz. Clausewitz said that 'war is the continuation of politics by other means'. That is, he believed that when politicians' discussions reached an impasse, their dispute passed onto the field of battle. This is a conventional way of understanding war. Foucault suggests saying that the reverse is true, that 'politics is war pursued by other means' (93/123). The idea here then is that when violent methods fail, we adopt peaceful ones, but ultimately peace or war are simply different modes of the struggle between forces. Peace is thus not the opposite of war, but a situation in which war continues, albeit in a relatively hidden way. Foucault is unsure that we should distinguish between war and politics at all. He thinks that the two things are just two different forms in which power coheres, 'two different strategies' for integrating force relations, but ones which are always prone to quickly switching back to the other form (93/123). This implies then that not only is peace more violent and chaotic than we ordinarily allow, but that war actually is more regular: war is not total chaos, but rather a heavily regulated state, which involves violence (as indeed does peace to some extent), but also large areas of peace, the organisation of areas behind the lines, the creation of order within an army, and also in certain ways a negotiation with the other side in manoeuvring, adhering to rules of war, etc.

This focus on war I think is the reason for the talk of 'force' here, although as I say it does not imply direct violence necessarily, so much as the pressure exerted by one's enemy's strength, which may work indirectly.

Foucault now switches into a more explicit listing of the features of power. This is in effect a list of conclusions that follow from the description of power he has already given us.

First on this list is a denial that power is the kind of thing one may be said to possess. We ordinarily talk in this way, about a particular individual having a lot of power, or being very powerful. For Foucault, this is at best a loose way of talking. There is no thing that a person actually has within themselves that makes them politically 'powerful', nor any real thing (say, some magic ring) someone can possess that gives 'power'. Rather, power comes from occupying a position in a complex social network that endows a person with power. This means that we may lose or gain power without losing or gaining any objects, and without changing in our own inherent qualities, because the context changes around us. Some changes of what we own or what we are may affect our social standing, but not necessarily. The point here is that power is not something you can possess like money, or an attribute you can have like strength or height, but something that consists essentially of relations you have to other people, which certainly have a lot to do with money and strength, but cannot be reduced to your property or attributes.

Secondly, Foucault deals with the connection of power 'to other types of relationship', specifically 'economic processes, relationships of knowledges, sexual relationships' (94/123*). Now, it is noteworthy that Foucault is in effect here extending the relational model that he is already using with power (though without yet explaining it fully) to several other areas. It is uncontentious to think of economics in terms of relationships (specifically relationships of exchange), or indeed sex (this being the most common use of the term 'relationship' today), but knowledge is not normally thought of as relational, but precisely something you either have or do not have. Foucault, however, here implies that it is relational, or at least that it has a relational aspect. This can be taken to mean, I think, for example, that if one person knows something and another does not, this may be said to be a form of knowledge relationship between them. My knowing something vis-à-vis your not knowing it is apt to create a power imbalance between us, moreover, and thus implies a power relationship. The power relationship then is, as Foucault says, not an optional extra tacked onto knowledge relations, but directly implied by them. Economic and sexual relationships too involve power relations. There is no economics or sex without contestation or forces pushing in this way and pulling in that. This then is Foucault's point about power in relation to other types of relationship: power is thus not a distinct thing in itself, but rather found immanently in all other types of relationship. The reverse can be said too: certainly all power relationships between people will have some impact on our knowledge, on our economic relationships and on our sexual ones. Moreover, much the same thing can be said of these types of relationship in general that can be said about power in general. Economics, sex and knowledge also constitute decentred networks that are ubiquitous in our society.

The idea that we cannot have sex without there being power involved might seem to make sex look quite sinister, but this is not Foucault's intention. Rather, his point is that power is ultimately banal and ubiquitous: it is so ordinary that in itself it is just part of life and not a bad thing to be opposed.

Thirdly, Foucault claims that 'power comes from below'. He initially explains this by reference to the absence of power from above: there is no pure ruler at the top. The full meaning, however, is that power, as we have seen, concatenates from local instances up to produce the great institutions and strategies. That is, the large-scale effects are dependent on their production from below and not vice versa. This does not imply that great institutions and strategies do not have effects on the local instances below them. It does imply, however, that although power has the capacity to link together lots of local power relations in strategic wholes, there remain 'wide effects of cleavage which run through the social body as a whole' (94/124). No matter what surface unities are generated by the interplay of power relations, this cannot then result in an end to the local instability and variability of power.

Foucault's fourth point here is the most surprising philosophically, namely that 'power relations are at one and the same time intentional and not subjective' (94/124*). This is an apparent philosophical paradox: intentionality, having intentions, having objects of one's intention, is normally the exclusive province of subjects, which is to say, traditionally, of conscious humans. Foucault here is not making the claim that power is an agent like a human being; this is why he says it is not a subject. However, power relations do have intentions, aims. How is this possible? In a word, one that Foucault does not use, since it has little currency as a concept in Foucault's time, this intentionality is *emergent*. This is a common effect noted in complex systems by the systems theory that has developed since Foucault's time: complex systems have emergent properties that are not found in their compositional elements. This emergence of properties can be seen even in very simple complexes. One example of emergence, it might be argued, is human intentionality itself: we are made up of molecules without intentionality, little chemical compounds that in themselves could do anything at all, but when put together and interacting with one another comprise a human being with full intentionality.

This subjective intentionality is the starting point for emergence of the intentionality of power. It is humans' intentional actions that concatenate into power with its intentions. Although power's intentionality derives from that of human agents, power's intentionality is emergent in this because it is different to that of the humans whose actions produce it. Power has different aims to the aims of people. This is the main point here: there is no one, not one person, who decides power's intentions. 'The logic is perfectly clear, the aims decipherable, and yet it happens that there is no one who devised them and few who express them' (95/125*). A few people might have exactly the same intentions as power, but this does not mean that these are the people in control. Power's intentionality perhaps derives from the intentions of powerful people to a disproportionate extent, but this does not mean it matches the intentions of those people exactly. Those who produce power effects are generally in ignorance of their existence and hence 'without hypocrisy', as Foucault puts it (95/125). The best example of this effect of emergent intentionality is, I think, the main figure of Foucault's previous book, *Discipline and Punish*. In that book, Foucault claims that the function of the prison system is to regularly produce recidivism, that is, to produce criminals. No one involved with shaping the prison system – not the guards, not the prisoners, not the bureaucrats, not the politicians, not the police – presumably actually has this goal in mind, and few if any people acknowledge its existence. Yet this is the unpalatable objective truth of the prison: locking people up actually causes criminality. This example I think can be taken as a paradigm of what Foucault means by a 'strategy' of power.

The fifth and last point on Foucault's list here is that 'where there is power, there is resistance and yet, or rather consequently, this resistance is never in a position of exteriority in relation to power' (95/125–6). This is an enormously difficult point, and a major target for criticism of Foucault. It is also a point of great practical importance, since, if his conception of power is to be useful, it will be from the point of view of mounting resistance to power. The space devoted to this point by Foucault belies its importance: even compared with his relatively scant remarks on power, he says almost nothing about its tenebrous opposite number, resistance.

The claim that where there is power there is resistance is straightforward, though it is not explained clearly within *The Will to Knowledge*. Foucault makes clear elsewhere that power engenders resistance since it is a matter of people being made to do things, and people quite naturally resist it.[32] The claim that resistance is not outside power, however, leads to a frequent interpretation of Foucault's position as being one that resistance is trapped within or produced by power, which is then taken to imply that he thinks that resistance is bound to fail. All force relations seem to generate power, so it is unclear how resistance can be different from any other power relation on Foucault's account. Thus any attempt to fight power would just seem to feed into its strategies. Perhaps we could say that one man's resistance is just another man's power.

Foucault here actually already anticipates such objections. He admits that we cannot 'escape' power, that we are always inside power. But in fact, since we can for Foucault resist within power, the fact that we cannot get outside of power is not a problem. This resistance is in effect the ability to intervene in the ensemble of power relations in order to alter them. That is not to say that resistance for Foucault consists in attempts to produce determinate outcomes deliberately in the ensemble of power relations. We actually have very little capacity for such deliberate political praxis on his account, since we do not understand what our actions produce at the levels of the strategies of power. Nevertheless, we can will resistance: we can resist something we do not like to get rid of it, not in order to establish some other definite alternative in its place. This entails that resistance is by its very nature not a great organised force opposing power. If power itself lacks any central organisation, then resistance too cannot have one, but rather arises locally in response to the specific phenomena of power. These may then take all kinds of forms (96/126). Though they are ubiquitous, their actual manifestation is irregular: resistance manifests at irregular intervals of space and time, in all kinds of unexpected ways, in different intensities, through different points of the body or emotions even. One form of the emergence of resistance is 'great radical ruptures', but this is atypical (96/127). Still, it is important to note that for Foucault resistances are far from being limited to localities: rather, they 'traverse social stratifications' (96/127). Thus, for Foucault, via 'the strategic codification of these points of resistance', revolution is possible as the outcome (96/127). While resistance might not be amenable to a grand central organisation, it nevertheless can be organised and targeted.

Summary
To summarise, power is:

- not centralised
- not made up of institutions
- not a form of or based in physical force
- not subjective

- not divided into distinct levels
- a continuum between war and politics
- relational
- fundamentally local, 'from below'
- immanent in all other kinds of relationship
- everywhere
- in continual flux, unstable, marked by cleavage
- emergently patterned
- intentional and strategic
- always occasioning resistance within it
- doubly conditioned by the reciprocal relations between different scales (the phrasing of this last point will be explained below).

These features of power mutually imply one another. Nothing here is contingent. Rather, Foucault has produced a total, coherent view of power. Power's relationality, for example, by itself leads to all the negative conclusions on the list: something that subsists in relations between people cannot be centralised, institutional, subjective, a form of force or divided into levels. It also implies that power comes from below, that there is a continuum between war and politics (the relations between people are fundamentally of the same type in either situation), that it is everywhere where people are, that it is unstable (since people are unstable), and that it always meets resistance (how this relates to relationality will be made clear below under 'Foucault's Later Views on Power: The Subject and Power'). The only thing that requires additional inference beyond relationality is the existence of emergent patterns, which are inherently surprising and require empirical knowledge to understand.

The simple idea of relationality applied here to produce almost this entire multifaceted conception is not new in Foucault's work.[33] Compare, for example, his 1966 statement on the nature of systems: 'By system, we must understand an ensemble of relations which are maintained and transformed independently of the things that they bind.'[34] If one replaces 'system' by 'power' in this statement, one gets the kernel of the conception of power Foucault articulates a decade later. Interestingly what he is doing in this extract, from an interview given right after the publication of his *Order of Things*, is effectively espousing what was often called a 'structuralist' point of view, invoking the theories of Georges Dumézil, Jacques Lacan and biological genetics as examples of the kind of analysis he was pursuing. Though he later distances himself from this paradigm, the model of the system seems to survive in his thought.

Foucault's Later Views on Power: The Subject and Power

Despite the apparent completeness of the view of power found in *The Will to Knowledge*, there is something manifestly lacking in it, which Foucault moves on to address, namely an account of how individual human subjects fit into it. Foucault is often accused, particularly in association with his work of the 1960s, of being radically opposed to the concept of the subject, but this accusation is exaggerated. Certainly, by the time of *The Will to Knowledge*, the subjective dimension figures in his analysis, though not as prominently as in more conventional social analysis. Foucault's account of power implies human subjects as the points between which power relations occur. However, the subject itself is portrayed by Foucault as something relatively passive, produced by confessional power. Questions are raised by this, specifically how the subject is constituted in relation to power, and how power is produced if it precedes the subject.

Foucault develops a positive account of subjectivity in the years after *The Will to Knowledge*. His initial approach centres around the notions of government and 'governmentality', the latter word coined by Foucault himself. It represents a shift from his concept of power-knowledge to a concern with 'governmental rationality', a way of governing that combines power and knowledge with subjectivity, a subject who governs and also subjects who are to be governed. Importantly, here, Foucault also insists that the notion of government can be applied reflexively; that is, we govern ourselves as well as others.

The development of this notion owes something to the trajectory of Foucault's historical researches during this period, specifically to his study of ancient thought. In ancient Greece and Rome the elite were very interested in 'techniques of the self', and linked these to politics: one must master oneself if one is to master others. It was at the time of these researches that Foucault wrote an extraordinary text, published as 'The Subject and Power', written half in French and half in English, which he provided as an appendix to a book written about him in close consultation with him, *Michel Foucault: Beyond Structuralism and Hermeneutics*, by two Americans, Paul Rabinow and Hubert Dreyfus. This appendix competes with the relevant chapters in *The Will to Knowledge* for the status of Foucault's major statement on the topic of power. I think it is most usefully read as an addendum to Foucault's earlier material on power, and effectively completes it.

The most important contribution of 'The Subject and Power' is a simple definition of power as a matter of 'actions upon the actions of others'.[35] Power is then a matter of a certain type of action, namely those which are designed to produce actions. This means that whenever we try to get someone to do something, we are engaging in power relations. Power is what happens through the concatenation of people influencing one another's behaviour. Self-evidently such actions are in a network of mutual incitement with one another: I act to get others to act, but the actions of others directed at my actions are implicated already in what I do. I am in a deep sense the product of the actions of others directed at changing my actions. I am also to this extent, however, also a product of my own actions, that is, of my own actions aimed at changing other actions of mine in turn. We exercise power on and within ourselves for Foucault; we constitute ourselves as subjects within and in relation to the network of power relations. This process is not the mere 'subjection' (*assujettissement*) he speaks of in *The Will to Knowledge*, our constitution by power, but what he will later call 'subjectivation', our self-constitution as subjects.

Criticisms

Foucault's views on power have been criticised by many people. However, these critics either misunderstand his views, or just recapitulate the very positions he rejects. He has been accused of giving much too great a role to power, of reducing everything to power, of making power the basis of society, or more minimally simply of making power something that is 'endogenous', capable of existing in itself. But he simply never makes any such claims, and indeed specifically disavows these claims in his original exposition of his views. His views are nevertheless widely rejected, for the obvious reason that they pointedly conflict with what everyone previously thought, and consequently must be rejected by anyone who wishes to maintain their previous views about politics. Many Marxists for example believe that economics is fundamental in some sense, a view that Foucault simply rejects by putting power on an equal basis with knowledge, economics, etc. From a Marxist perspective this means that Foucault is putting much too much emphasis on both power and knowledge, but this is really just a basic disagreement between two perspectives.

Liberals, including liberal Marxists and neo-Marxists, have found themselves at odds with Foucault over his rejection of any kind of moral framework. From a liberal point of view, it is important to differentiate between bad, illegitimate, repressive power and the good liberation from this that they champion. For Foucault, things are rather more complicated. Power cannot be said to be a bad thing in itself for him, because it is so ubiquitous and often banal. Foucault does clearly support resistance against power, but resistance is not opposed to power per se, meaning that the lines are blurred in terms of what one should support and condemn. For his critics, this is a slippery slope Foucault is on, such that as soon as the clear difference is lost politics has been abolished.

Particularly important critiques of Foucault from this liberal direction include Charles Taylor's 'Foucault on Freedom and Truth' and Lecture X of Jürgen Habermas's *Philosophical Discourse of Modernity*. For Taylor, the lack of clear distinction between power and resistance in Foucault's schema simply indicates a lack of clarity in Foucault's thought, by which he has suppressed his liberal moral preference for resistance because he pedantically insists on a Nietzschean amoralism. Doubtless, this is how Foucault's thought will look if one believes in universal, moral political principles. From Foucault's perspective, however, such a universal moralism is dangerous, because it is liable to feed into strategies of power, due to the complicated relation between humans' intentions and the intentionality of power. Foucault's historical studies show that normative frameworks are not transhistorical, and that any attempt to posit them sees us stuck within a strategy of power and historical frame. He is trying to do something altogether more radical than moral critique, namely to appeal to the movement underneath history by which norms arise, to look at the indices of historical transformation as such. This of course cannot hope to completely break the bounds of historical location, but it does allow oneself to think beyond the historical situation in which one finds oneself.

Habermas accuses Foucault of three things: (1) presentism (seeing himself as trapped in the perspective of the present); (2) relativism (seeing his analyses as products of the present); (3) arbitrary partisanship (providing no explanation at all for taking the positions that he takes). Foucault in fact is not guilty on any of these counts. For him there is no pure present, and his work is an attempt to think outside the present by reference to what is not the present (namely the past), in an attempt to see beyond the present. He is thus not relativist at all in the sense

Habermas suggests, since Foucault's whole enterprise is an attempt to break out of the current way of seeing things, such as the repressive hypothesis.[36] Therefore, his position is not one of arbitrary partisanship, which would imply choosing one of the currently available views and adhering to that position for no explicit reason. Foucault's mission on the contrary is to produce a new position, and to do this not by picking sides but by criticising whatever he finds in the present. Critique is the side that Foucault takes, a negative operation founded in a sense on the things it criticises, but always exceeding them.

The misunderstanding here I think is tied up with a failure to appreciate the radicalness of Foucault's notion of power. For Habermas, Foucault is a sociological 'functionalist', who thinks of society as an organic whole in which everything has its function. This seems manifestly false, inasmuch as, at least theoretically, Foucault thinks of society as in a continual state of flux and war with itself. It is possible that he thinks in functional terms at certain points, and he does talk about function in relation to power at points. However, his overall position is clearly that society is marked by coherent patterns of power – strategies – which interrelate, rather than seeing society itself as such as an integrated system.

Methodological Conclusions

Having given us his account of power, Foucault returns in Chapter 2 of Part Four to the question of sex, which he only mentions intermittently in passing during that account (97/128). The principal consequence of his reconception of power for the history of sexuality is that sexuality cannot have been deliberately produced by some powerful agency. Given Foucault's account of power, the question is rather how sexuality has been produced from below. This does not mean, however, he notes, simply referring to all the individual events that happen in relation to sex, that is, simply to diffuse occurrences at a local level (97–8/129). It is rather the emergence of patterns that concerns him. To answer this question, we must first answer a complicated set of questions about the interrelation of discourses and power, the interplay of power and resistance, as well as the role of institutions and the state. Foucault has already answered these questions, however.

He concludes the chapter by attending to its purported theme, method. He expounds four methodological rules to guide the remainder of his study of sexuality:

1. 'Rule of immanence': the idea here is that power is immanent to sexuality. We cannot have knowledge about sexuality without power being in play, Foucault points out; discourses concerning sexuality are already imbued with power. The point for him here is then, he says, to find nodal points of power-knowledge, where power and knowledge meet, such as confession, or the body of the child, and use these as the backbone of his account.

2. 'Rules of continual variations': what we look at is not who occupies what position in some structure, but what the patterns of transformation are in the dynamic system. What is important for Foucault is not who has how much power at a given time, but what processes happen over time. This for Foucault is what relations of power-knowledge are about: not forming a static distribution, but governing transformations. The example Foucault gives here is of the relationship of the family to the medical profession, of how something that began with the doctor called in by the adults to examine the child's sexuality morphs into a situation where the doctor calls into question the sexuality of the parents (99/131).

3. 'Rule of double conditioning': this deals with the relationship of the local to the larger scale. Foucault's point here is that the two affect or 'condition' each other. Foucault denies moreover that there is any discontinuity between the two, or that they constitute 'levels' (99–100/132). That does not mean that things are simply the same at different scales – Foucault reiterates now his earlier denial that the power of the state simply repeats the power of the father at a larger scale. Indeed, his denial that power has 'levels' implies that there cannot be a repetition of this kind, but rather that things are all part of a continuum where power is concerned. What happens on one scale only affects what happens on another, but does not determine it. This means that there is no particular implication of what is happening at the small scale, for example, to what is happening at the larger, or vice versa. Foucault gives us the example of the family unit as a cohesive and relatively independent structure. This was produced by power involving factors at different scales, but once produced it could be slotted into various different strategies at a larger scale.

4. 'Rule of the tactical polyvalence of discourses' (100/132): 'tactical polyvalence' is the nub of this point. 'Polyvalence' is the property of being able to combine in many ways. Foucault's point here is that

discourses can combine with various other discourses according to the tactical situation. We are used to seeing discourses as relating to one another at a logical or lexical level. If the claims made in one discourse oppose those made in another, we take them to be opposed to one another. While this is true at a superficial, lexical level, tactically they may, however, be complementary. An example from *Discipline and Punish* is the polyvalence of discourses advocating the reform of prisons and those advocating harsher punishments: the two cohere in supporting the prison system itself as such. The point here is that you simply cannot tell from looking at the content of the arguments used what the political function of the discourse is. The only way to discern what effects discourses have is to analyse their operation in practice. We cannot presume that a discourse, or even a fragment of a discourse, operates in the same way in different times and places, or when uttered by different persons or in different contexts. The same can be said of silences (101/133). Discourse is not then to be divided only into allowed and excluded, or dominant and dominated. Both silences and discourses can rather in different contexts be means either of strengthening power or of resisting it. Foucault's example here is homosexuality. The invention and application of homosexuality as a medical category was obviously initially used to pathologise and persecute homosexuals, but then homosexuals themselves took over the notion of homosexuality as a positive category with which they identified to demand their liberation: we are homosexual by nature, they said, so do not punish us for that. There are then for Foucault two 'levels' we have to look at in relation to discourses to analyse their role: firstly, 'their tactical productivity (what reciprocal effects of power and knowledge they ensure)' and secondly, 'their strategic integration' (what strategies they operate in) (102/135). In the case of homosexuality, we have a discourse that has been turned to opposite tactical purposes at different moments. The initial effects of the labelling of people as 'homosexuals' were their transformation into abnormal subjects to be medicalised. Later, this label was turned tactically to a different purpose, to end the vilification of homosexuals. However, both tactics occur within and support the same basic strategy: sexuality. For this reason, Foucault thinks we should remain wary of the label of homosexuality.

This notion of tactical polyvalence I think can be applied not only to discourses, but also, though Foucault does not say this, to strategies of power themselves, and the way they relate to one another, to behaviours, to power relations: all these things are fundamentally promiscuous on Foucault's account.

The Distribution of Sexuality (Part Four, Chapters 3–4)

Chapter 3

The third chapter of Part Four is entitled 'Domain'. The domain in question is that of 'the device of sexuality' invoked in the title of Part Four. This chapter is thus about the spatial distribution of the device.

It begins: 'Sexuality must not be described as a restive upsurge, alien by nature and unruly by necessity towards a power which, for its part, exhausts itself to subdue sexuality and often fails to master it entirely' (103/136*). The claim here is that sexuality is not natural, nor does it have its own native force independently of power. It is 'rather a particularly dense crossing point for power relations', that is, a point where all kinds of social power relations meet (103/136*). It is thus not repressed by power, but rather extraordinarily productive in terms of power effects, usable in all kinds of strategies. There is indeed no single strategy of power where sex is concerned. Sexuality's importance then is not that it belongs to a single hegemonic form, but that it is extraordinarily politically malleable. For this reason, there can be no simple account of the political dimension of sexuality, such as is offered by the repressive hypothesis. Rather, says Foucault, there are 'beginning in the eighteenth century, four great strategic ensembles' (103/137* – Hurley has Foucault calling these 'unities', whereas Foucault's *ensembles* I think implies something less than unitary):

1. '*A hysterization of women's bodies*': a strategy peculiarly focused on women, taking their bodies to be especially sexual compared with men's, disqualifying women from some things while giving them a special status in other respects (104/137*). Women's sexuality was declared to be a lurking pathology (namely 'hysteria' – literally this refers to a disease emanating from a woman's uterus [*hystera* in Greek], but came to be seen as simply a distinct nervous disorder afflicting women), while women are simultaneously given special responsibility for producing the next generation.

2. '*A pedagogization of children's sex*': a paradoxical strategy by which

children are simultaneously asserted to be invariably sexual and naturally sexless (104/137–8*). That is, it is noted that children all engage in sexual behaviour, but at the same time this is deemed completely inappropriate. The consequence is a major attempt to 'educate' the sexuality of children in the appropriate direction, involving families, doctors, schools and ultimately even psychologists.

3. '*A socialization of procreative behavior*': by which sexual reproduction became society's business, a collective, economic concern, and hence a political question (104–5/138*); sex itself becomes a question of public policy, and 'family planning' a matter for state action.

4. '*A psychiatrization of perverse pleasure*': sexuality is categorised as a separate biological and psychological entity, hence a distinct domain of psychiatric medicine. All its possible disorders are catalogued, and remedies applied (105/138*).

All these strategies contribute to a single effect, the 'production of sexuality' (105/139). Hurley uses the phrase 'a historical construct' to translate Foucault's description of this, but Foucault actually calls it *un dispositif historique*, a historical *device*. That is not to say it is not constructed, but Foucault does not say here that it is in as many words. The problem with the word 'construct' is that it might be taken to imply that there is some agent doing the construction, when for Foucault there is none. What is right about using the phrase 'historical construct' is the implication that, for Foucault, there is nothing natural about sexuality (105/139).

This historicity of sexuality is a major stumbling block for readers: how can we understand sexuality as something historically invented? Have not people always been sexual? Foucault will offer answers to these questions in Part Five.

For now he contrasts this device of sexuality with another historical device, the 'device of alliance' (*dispositif d'alliance* – Hurley here translates *dispositif* as 'deployment', losing the contrast that Foucault is here talking about two different *dispositifs*; 106/140*). This device, according to Foucault, has arisen in every society. That is, in every society, sexual relationships have existed and played a political role in ties of alliance between groups (106/140). Such systems of kinship can reach great levels of complexity and are a mainstay of anthropological study.

Foucault contrasts the devices of alliance and sexuality 'term by term': alliance is based on rules dividing what is allowed from what is forbidden, whereas sexuality is organised around variable 'techniques of power'; the former is about links between persons, whereas the latter is about individuals themselves (106/140). Both devices are linked to economics, but in different ways. The device of alliance, Foucault claims, is 'in a word' about 'the homeostasis of the social body', which is to say, about maintaining social stability (107/141). It is for this reason, he says, that it is linked to the law. Alliance functions through the enforcement of laws concerning obligations in sexual relationships, and the exclusion of the forbidden, passing through the power of public authority, to reinforce the social order. Sexuality, by contrast, is about the control of bodies, and of populations. How these concerns differ from those of alliance will be explained below.

Foucault here proposes certain 'theses' contrary to the repressive hypothesis (Hurley calls these 'hypotheses', but this is not the word Foucault uses, and I think it is significant that he chooses to use a different word for his position to that used to describe the repressive hypothesis, for reasons already covered above; 107/141*). His theses are that sexuality (1) is 'tied to recent devices of power' (107/141); (2) has been expanding at an increasing rate since the eighteenth century (the translation gives 'seventeenth', but it is eighteenth in Foucault's original French); (3) is not fundamentally about reproduction; (4) is always associated with the 'intensification of the body' in terms of knowledge and power (107/141*). We have already seen Foucault argue for (3) especially, but (1) and (4) in particular remain for him to demonstrate. All are at stake in the device of sexuality, this recent device of power that has, according to Foucault, been increasing its rate of expansion ever since it first appeared on the scene.

The rise of the device of sexuality in the West saw a concomitant decline in the importance of the device of alliance: the political constraints imposed on sexual relationships declined (one thinks most obviously of the legalisation of divorce), as has the general social and economic importance of such relationships (106/140). The newer device does not *replace* the older one, however. Though Foucault thinks that might one day happen, the two have up till now operated in tandem.

Indeed, Foucault argues that sexuality originally came into existence out of and on the basis of the device of alliance (107/142). As we have seen, confession, so central to the formation of sexuality, was initially a practice focused on questions about the marital relationship, the crux of the device of alliance, which later expanded beyond this function. This transition from alliance to sexuality was made via a thematic common to both devices, namely a concern with the '"flesh"', Foucault argues. This 'flesh' essentially referred to the body and pleasure, which were already a focus in confession before sexuality, and which constituted the basis of sexuality in turn. The family, moreover, remains a focus throughout the transition. It indeed provides a shared locus that integrates the two devices. The family, Foucault insists, is not only central to alliance, but is also 'anchoring' sexuality today (108/143*).

Though the family is a privileged site of sexuality, however, it is not where sexuality originated. It does seem to be, Foucault says, but he compares the family to a refracting crystal, which only reflects light coming from outside (111/147). He argues instead that the device of sexuality developed 'on the margins of familial institutions' and then moved into the family itself (110/145*). The agency of this invasion of the family was medical: family relations were '"psychologized" or "psychiatrized"' (110/146). The pretext for sexuality's advance into the family was one of reinforcing the old system of alliance. Figures that failed to perform their roles within the system of alliance – bad mothers, bad fathers, bad children – were all diagnosed as having sexual disorders, such as homosexuality, hysteria or sexual precociousness. Pursuing these dysfunctions of family life, medics inevitably found a sexuality in the midst of the family that was viewed as a cancer threatening to destroy the family, and with it the system of alliance, and hence society itself. For Foucault, however, this sexuality was not simply something that existed in the family prior to their investigations, that the psychiatrists then rooted out, as those investigators thought at the time. Rather, it has been imposed by precisely the interventions that appear to discover it. This imposition did not merely take the form of direct intervention, but more widely, families were now urgently enjoined from without to monitor the dangerous sexuality lurking within. Each of the 'four great strategies' listed above is now thus implemented via the family (114/150).

The convergence of the two devices, sexuality and alliance, on the family, however, creates a particularly problematic effect. From the point of view of alliance, sex within the family is forbidden (apart from between the married couple), hence there have long been laws against incest. However, the reason for this is relatively banal: incest is pointless since it can produce no useful political effect, because members of a family are already allied to one another. Alliance proceeds from marriages between different families. The more serious taboo from the point of view of alliance was sex outside marriage, particularly adultery, since it threatens the institution of marriage. Sexuality's entry into the family, however, incites a maelstrom of sexual feelings within it, which threatens to break out in incest, and thus to destroy the family as the basis of alliance. The coexistence of the two devices here requires that this not be allowed. Hence, incest is viewed as a greater danger than ever, since there is now both a greater risk of it occurring and because its occurrence will threaten the very integration of the two devices. As the importance of alliance diminishes, adultery ceases to be such a concern, and incest becomes the major taboo. Our society insists on the prohibition as no society ever has before, including insisting that this prohibition is a universal rule that has applied in all societies throughout history (109/144–5). Foucault thus characterises modern anthropology's claim that the incest taboo is a transcultural constant as a support for the device of sexuality (110/145). That said, in a sense his own view would predict that a ban on incest would be ubiquitous to historical societies, since Foucault himself thinks that alliance has existed in all of them. The point is rather that the explanation of the incest taboo in terms of a natural and universal abhorrence of incest is wrong, a position that asserts that incest is unthinkable – which indeed for our society it largely would be due to the political stakes involved on Foucault's account.

Foucault details attempts by psychiatrists to negotiate this problem of sexuality in the family. Firstly, he describes Charcot's practice of removing the patient from the family, which Foucault understands in terms of a separation of sexuality (in the person of the patient) from alliance (the family). The family would bring the patient to the doctor, having been enjoined to watch out for sexual abnormality, and having then detected it in one of their number. When the doctor took the patient away from the family, the family would clamour for the patient back – but Charcot responds that the removal is for the good of the family, so that the patient can be cured and then returned to its bosom (112/148). As we have seen in the example of Salpêtrière above, Charcot had a certain reticence about sex, and maintained a silence around the sexual dimension of this problem of removing people too.

His approach is superseded by psychoanalysis, which dispenses with this reticence, but retains a certain crucial division. Like Charcot, the analysts remove patients from the family in order to restore them to the family in a healthy state, but they do it only for brief daily sessions. Quite unlike Charcot, their means for curing the patient is precisely to talk about sex in the frankest possible manner.

It is only here, most of the way through the book, that Foucault for the first time discusses psychoanalysis directly. I think, however, that psychoanalysis has never been far from the surface of Foucault's analysis, in multiple ways. The repressive hypothesis was clearly at least significantly influenced by psychoanalysis, for example, though it explicitly rejects psychoanalysis ultimately. Psychoanalysis is surely the combination of sex and confession par excellence, moreover. In this chapter too psychoanalysis has up to this point been lurking: the continual invocation of the relationship between the family and sexuality calls psychoanalysis to mind immediately, given Freud's signature theory that psychological problems primarily emanate from the difficulties people have in negotiating the sexual desire they had for their parents as children.

Psychoanalysis thus discovers the family structure to be embedded at the deepest level of the mind, in the form of the Oedipus complex, and therefore as a transhistorical constant. It therefore represents the most complete accommodation between the device of alliance and that of sexuality. Foucault thinks, however, that this is in effect a failure to understand what is really happening in relation to power, to understand where the psychic forms have come from.

The psychoanalytic treatment isolates the patient from the family, but does not remove them for longer than an hour, and in fact assures them that the only way to get better is to accept and explore the importance of familial relations (113/149). In particular, Foucault refers here to the connection of alliance to desire by psychoanalysis: without the family attachments, without its rules, psychoanalytic theory asserts, we can have no desire. Though this can serve as a description of psychoanalysis in general, it seems once again that Foucault is specifically alluding to its Lacanian form, which is so uniquely focused on desire, and holds that desire can only develop through an encounter with what Lacan calls 'the law'.

Foucault's position here is redolent of the repressive hypothesis's criticism of Freud's treatment as normalising, though Foucault of course is criticising Freud for protecting both alliance and sexuality, whereas the repressive hypothesis sees Freud as defending the family against sexuality.

In the penultimate paragraph of the chapter, Foucault returns to the repressive hypothesis. This is an extraordinarily tricky paragraph to understand: for one thing, it is essentially ironic, and there is no clear indication of this in the English version; secondly, because there is a subtle error in the translation; and thirdly, because Foucault's sarcasm is conveyed through the use of obscure technical vocabulary.

Foucault starts here by talking about a 'moment' of the history of sexuality which 'would correspond to the necessity of constituting a "labour force"' (114/150*). Hurley's error is to miss out the 'would', the fact that the verb is in the conditional. The English version thus has Foucault actually saying this on his own account, but in the original Foucault uses the conditional case for the main verbs throughout the paragraph, unlike in the preceding or following paragraphs, indicating that he is not speaking so directly or literally.

The moment referred to here by Foucault is one posited in the repressive hypothesis at the beginning of the book, at which it is held that sex has been repressed, to the end of producing the workforce required by early capitalism. He now adds to this a second moment, one identified with a slackening of repression. This moment, Foucault refers to with the German phrase *Spätkapitalismus* (114/150). This phrase, meaning 'late capitalism', has a decidedly Marxist complexion, since it implies that capitalism is today near its end. It is particularly closely associated with the thinkers of the Frankfurt School, to refer to a capitalism in a subtler phase, doing away with grinding poverty in favour of harnessing workers as consumers. The implication of such a view is that even though sexuality has been liberated, it is nevertheless assumed as a point of purchase for contemporary capitalism.

Foucault here uses the extraordinary phrase *désublimation sur-répressive*, translated by Hurley as 'hyperrepressive desublimation' (114/151). What does this phrase mean? This requires some forensic reconstruction. 'Sublimation' is a term employed in psychoanalytic theory to refer to the diversion of libido to a particular object. *De*sublimation then is the reverse of this process, the detachment of desire from its original object. 'Repressive desublimation' is a concept found, although not in a very developed way, in a particular work, Herbert Marcuse's *One-Dimensional Man*. Marcuse complains that there is today a general desublimation, whereby the product of sublimation, culture, declines. While such a desublimation might seem like liberation, Marcuse thinks it is actually repressive. The full phrase *désublimation sur-répressive*, or its English or German translations, is not found anywhere but in Foucault's own work, however, even though Foucault here implies that others have used it. It seems to be a combination of Marcuse's 'repressive desublimation' with a different concept of Marcuse's 'surplus repression' (*sur-répression* in French), which he uses in *Eros and Civilization*. *Surplus* repression for Marcuse is the form of repression that occurs beyond that necessary to constitute society.[37]

The idea that desublimation is surplus-repressive (which Marcuse does not put forward, since he used the concepts of surplus repression and desublimation at different moments of his career) is a kind of pastiche of Marcuse's position, combining with a concept, *Spätkapitalismus*, which he personally rejected, though he was close to the members of the Frankfurt School who did use it. Thus, Foucault seems to be satirising a certain kind of German neo-Marxism. This satire is actually quite brilliant in relation to Marcuse. The combination of his two concepts in effect shows the problem with the notion of surplus repression, and indeed his use of the term repression to describe desublimation. It is clear that desublimation does not proceed via an excess of repression, or indeed via repression at all.

Foucault's conclusion of the chapter is to note that to do the history of sex in terms of these two moments is inadequate.

Chapter 4

This chapter is called 'periodisation', and in it Foucault seeks to explain how we might conceive the chronological dimension of the device of sexuality, adding this to the spatial dimension explored in the previous chapter. If we read the history of sexuality as centred on repression, one finds 'two ruptures' in it (115/152), the two-moments view rejected at the end of the previous chapter. We see the beginning of a serious repression during the seventeenth century, with the restriction of sexuality to the marital couple. Then we see repression loosening (Foucault in fact indicates that this would not have been a rupture so much as gradual change), the 'sexual revolution' with which we are all familiar, during which things were seen, talked about and legalised which had previously been forbidden. Foucault proposes to subvert this repressive view (yet again), by closely reconstructing the chronology of the methods involved, which he thinks will not support this neat two-phase history.

The next paragraph begins with the number 1. without an explanation as to why. Several pages follow before the number 2. appears, which is the end of the list. Foucault does not make it very clear what is being numbered here. It would seem that number 1. introduces a basic 'chronology of techniques' (115/153*), whereas 2. deals with the history of their actual application.

The techniques in question are those of confession, birthed in the medieval Church, then intensifying from the sixteenth century in parallel development in both Protestantism and Catholicism, up to the end of the eighteenth century (116/153). He indicates that the two parallel tendencies terminate in 'Alfonso de' Liguori' in the Catholic case and 'Wesleyan pedagogy' in Protestantism. He in fact refers to this dyad twice, in different places (116/153; 120/159). Alphonsus Liguori, as he is known in English (Hurley gives the Italian version of his name, whereas Foucault gives the French), was an Italian contemporary of the English father of Methodism, John Wesley. It would seem indeed that Liguori is roughly the equivalent of Wesley in that century in their respective cults, both major revitalisers founding their own movements (Liguori's was the Redemptorists). It is not immediately obvious, however, why either is so important for Foucault, given that he is tracing the history of confession, and neither figure was especially associated with any form of confession, although in *Abnormal* Foucault credits Liguori with being the one who took confession from acts to intentions.[38] John Wesley we associate with an Arminian belief in the possibility of salvation for anyone, together with a belief that moral perfection is attainable in this life. The Redemptorists similarly believe in the redeemability of sinners, hence their name. I would suggest that this common universal mission explains why they are important for Foucault: they urge the universal application of religious techniques, including confession in the broad sense of the personal and public examination of one's conduct. The reference to pedagogy is also a clue. Wesley was concerned with improving the quality and discipline of education, both in religious and secular instruction, which ties into the development of discipline in education posited by Foucault.

At this point a 'new technology of sex' appeared (116/154). What was new about this was primarily that it was outside of the Church, though it was not entirely different in its normative moral categories. This technology operated through secular state institutions – 'pedagogy, medicine, and economics' – which provided three new 'axes' for expansion (116/154).

How do these three axes relate to the four strategies elaborated earlier? I think we can say that three of the strategies relate particularly to certain axes: the strategy in relation to children is pursued through pedagogy, and socialisation relates to economics, and medicine is the locus of psychiatrisation. The hysterisation of women can be said to occur at the meeting point of all three axes, with women providing the bodies through which society is reproduced, the primary carers of children, as well as being pathologised subjects in their own right.

In each axis, groundwork had already been laid by Christianity: the sexuality of children was a concern in a Church that provided the primary forms of institutional pedagogy in Europe for over a thousand years; medical psychology emerged in an area previously the domain of religious concern with possession (though clearly with a fundamentally different ontology); demographic regulation builds on the Church's ministrations to the married couple (117/154–5). One could add, to extend this point to the fourth strategy, that the Church had long been suspicious of women.

From the beginning of the nineteenth century, the focus on death, and eternal punishment and reward, gave way to a focus on life and health. The 'flesh' is no longer understood as a sinful vessel, but an organism (117/155). This led in two directions medically in respect of sex. Firstly, there was a concern with a specifically sexual area of disorder. The does not mean sexually transmitted disease, nor does it refer purely to psychological phenomena, but rather to diseases of the whole organism that affect sexuality, a category that does not exist in medicine any more. The idea then was that sexual abnormality was indicative of some underlying malady specifiable only through the sexual behaviour. Secondly, there was a new concern with the heritability of traits, which related to sex as the route by which anything is inherited. This concern led in the direction of eugenics (118/156). The two concerns combine in a concern about 'degenerescence', that is that sexual perversion is itself inheritable or leads to defects in offspring, or that sexual perversion is itself the outcome of bad breeding. 'The perversion-heredity-degenerescence ensemble constituted the solid nucleus of the new technologies of sex' (118/157*).

This clearly has not lasted to the present day. Foucault locates a 'rupture' of this 'system' with psychiatry at the end of the nineteenth century. At this point the concern with perversion was detached from the concern with heredity. Foucault credits Freud and psychoanalysis with this (119/157). There is a noteworthy error in the translation here, with the phrase 'position of psychiatry' appearing where Foucault in fact is talking about the position of *psychoanalysis* (see the Glossary below for an explanation of the difference).

Foucault's history of ruptures is different to that offered by the repressive hypothesis. It is a history of the production and invention of new things, rather than an imposition of repression followed by a gradual lifting. It is dominated by two major productive moments: the innovation of confessional techniques in the sixteenth century and the growth of psychiatric ones in the nineteenth.

Having dated the invention of techniques under point 1., Foucault now examines their application under point 2. (120–1/158). He notes that the technologies were applied first to the privileged, and only later spread more widely. This is true for medieval confession as for modern psychoanalysis. Models of family conduct produced in the privileged classes are later generalised throughout society. The woman who was hysterised, the child who was paradoxically sexualised, were initially those of the privileged class. There is a logic to this: it was the privileged women and children who were idle and thus likely to spend their time in hysteria or onanism, and who had the money to pay doctors to make them the objects of medical attention, at a time when ordinary people could scarcely afford medical care even for the most serious afflictions. This undercuts the Marxist inflexion of the repressive hypothesis: far from being an attempt to produce pliant workers, sexuality was initially confined to those who were well outside the working class.

There is continuity here with the older device of alliance. While that device held sway throughout medieval society, it must have preeminently been a consideration of the privileged class, the aristocracy, for whom alliances were of vital importance. It certainly would have mattered to peasants whom their children married, but to the aristocrat, connections of blood and marriage were the primary route to power in a hierarchy of inheritance. The technology of the Church too was devoted disproportionately to ministering to the great, and to those relatively privileged people who were part of the Church itself. Confession was thus a regular practice for the elite before it ever was for the ordinary laity.

According to Foucault, the application of sexuality to the masses began with the discovery of the existence of forms of birth control among the lower orders (121/161). This apparently caused moral outrage on the basis that the common people were assumed to be more natural than the higher orders, hence should not cheat nature like this. We should remember also that Foucault has already indicated that political concern with sex comes from a concern with the natality of the people, hence it may be taken that the outrage at popular birth control was also related to a political desire to increase the population, which these home prophylactics would be seen as retarding. Such material considerations are explicitly posited by Foucault in describing the next phase of the introduction of sexuality to the masses. This is the establishment of the '"conventional" family' 'around the eighteen-thirties, as an indispensable instrument of political control and economic regulation of the urban proletariat' (122/161). That is, a model of family life practised among the well-to-do was at this time imposed quite deliberately on the working class, precisely in order to allow the working class to be better regulated. The previous arrangements of the urban poor – informal associations, living in extended groups – were considered too messy, as well as immoral. The third and final phase that Foucault identifies was the imposition of the medical and juridical control of perversions on the whole of society at the end of the nineteenth century. It is as an example of this phase that the treatment of the rural simpleton is so important for Foucault.

With this, sexuality came to be spread through the whole of society, though in a variegated way. Repression was not uniform across society, nor indeed did it exist across the whole of society (122/161). For the upper classes who first introduced sexuality, it was not a matter of repression, but of 'intensification' (122–3/162). Repression was not on their agenda: they did not invent sexuality so as to repress themselves. Rather, they wanted health, life and strength (123/162). Thus the bourgeoisie was not concerned to 'disqualify' its genitalia (*sexe* – see Glossary below; 123/163*), not to castrate itself, but was rather obsessed with this part of its body, indeed making the entire body subordinate to it. Their whole future in effect is taken to depend on their genitals as the organ by which they reproduce. The bourgeoisie 'invested' 'its own sex with a technology of power and knowledge which it had itself invented', thereby emphasising the value of its body and pleasures. This same device, invented for these purposes, later came to be a tool for 'economic control and political subjection' when applied more widely to the lower classes (123/163*).

Here, Foucault seems to be separating out the repressive from the productive moments of sexuality's application, by putting the imposition of sexuality on the lower orders on the one side and the invention of sexuality by the wealthy on the other. It would seem indeed that here Foucault is not refuting the class analysis of the repressive hypothesis, so much as the direction it gives to the class dimension: where the repressive hypothesis thinks that sexual repression is the tool of the bourgeoisie, Foucault turns this around and declares that it is sexuality itself that is its tool. It is worth noting that Foucault puts 'ruling classes' here in scare quotes (122/162). This is doubtless because his account of power in earlier chapters of this part of the book does not allow that power can be fully concentrated in the hands of a particular class. The Marxist terms 'bourgeoisie' (meaning in French the burghers, the town-dwellers, but acquiring the meaning in Marxism of the capitalist class, the new urban ruling class under capitalism) and 'proletariat' (literally those who breed in Latin, the lower orders), however, appear without scare quotes. That is, Foucault acknowledges the reality of class division here in Marxist terms, but does not allow that this is a hierarchical arrangement of 'rule' of one class over others. Still, Foucault allows that the bourgeoisie are in a sense the masters and the beneficiaries of sexuality, and that the proletariat are conversely more repressed by it than the bourgeoisie.

The nobility, the 'ruling' class before the bourgeoisie came to power, had a different focus of attention, namely '*blood*' (124/164). Status for them derived from blood, which is to say from ancestry. This concern superficially resembles the biological preoccupations of the bourgeoisie, but while strength of the individual was certainly supposed in the Middle Ages to correlate to strong ancestry, what was important for the nobles was simply to be descended from someone great and inherit their rights and special status. For the bourgeoisie, by contrast, what was important was the specific health of the individual qua organism, so that it was a matter of breeding the superior biological specimen (124/165). Heredity became a more complicated matter. One must be careful what hereditary diseases might lurk in the family tree of one's spouse, for example. One could contrast this bourgeois concern with health with the proclivity for inbreeding among European royal families even though it led to congenital diseases. Foucault (125/166) links this new attitude to heredity to 'racism', though he does not really explain the link until Part Five.

The bourgeoisie, Foucault thinks, constitute themselves as a class via an affirmation of the body. This distinguishes them from the class they strive to replace, the aristocracy, who continue to be obsessed with the heraldry of their ancestry even while their place in society is usurped by the new class. The valorisation of the body also distinguished the bourgeoisie from the proletariat, the class that the bourgeoisie lived by exploiting, whose bodies and indeed lives had no importance for the bourgeoisie. Foucault speaks of 'conflicts' here as bringing the

bourgeoisie to recognise the proletariat's body. In doing so, he acknowledges something like the Marxist notion of class struggle, by which the
social order is the outcome of contention between classes. Some of
the things Foucault notes seem indeed to imply such contention, such
as conflicts over urban space: these seem to imply that the proletariat
simply asserted themselves by demanding space and the bourgeoisie
were compelled to acknowledge their presence as a consideration in
their own modus vivendi. Other factors he lists seem to imply conflict
of a different order, such as disease. The fact that proletarians could
get diseases that could be passed on to their betters certainly forced the
latter to be concerned with what was happening inside the bodies of the
former, though without the proletarians in this case necessarily demanding it. Prostitution is mentioned here by Foucault, no doubt because this
was a specific point of intimate contact between bourgeois and proletarians in which diseases could pass from the latter to the former. There
were larger-scale concerns too, touching on the essential relationship
between the two classes: the bourgeoisie needed the proletariat to be
an effective labour force in their industries, so actually had an interest
in the workers' welfare. This led the bourgeoisie to shift radically from
ignoring the physicality and sexuality of workers to administering both
their bodies and their sex through a range of institutions in which these
things were closely controlled: schools, public housing, hospitals, welfare
(126/167–8).

This in turn, thinks Foucault, meant that the proletariat tended to
resist sexuality in toto (127/168). On this point Foucault thinks there
has been a mistake (associated, of course, with the repressive hypothesis),
in which people have criticised the bourgeoisie for repressing sexuality,
and then in turn thinking that the proletariat's resistance to sexuality is
a form of subservience to 'bourgeois morality'. On the contrary, thinks
Foucault, what is bourgeois is sexuality, and proletarian resistance to it
is just that.

Readers may be confused here to see Foucault describing sexuality
as emanating from a bourgeois 'hegemonic center', given his view that
power does not have a centre. This is indeed a mistranslation: Foucault
actually says that sexuality spreads from a hegemonic home (a *foyer
hégémonique*), which describes the bourgeois context aptly, since it is both
culturally hegemonic and the place that sexuality originated (127/169*).

The bourgeoisie deliberately seek to differentiate their sexuality from
that of the poor from the end of the nineteenth century, in order, as

Foucault puts it, to 'protect its body' (128/169). It is here Foucault thinks that the 'theory of repression' comes into play (128/169). The reference here is, again, to psychoanalysis and its claim that some form of repression of sexuality is necessary to civilisation. This theory allows the classes to be differentiated from one another on the basis that, although everyone is now acknowledged as sexual, repression operates differentially on the sexuality of different classes.

According to Foucault, psychoanalysis provides a theory of the universality of sexuality, which reassures us that sexuality's spread through society is natural, while also inscribing the law and repression within sexuality, hence making the linkage of sexuality with government policy seem natural too. Though Foucault perhaps thinks it too obvious to bother pointing this out, noting only that psychoanalysis is a 'limited therapeutic practice' (130/172), psychoanalysis was initially developed as a treatment for the wealthy, indeed primarily for the treatment of the nervous disorders developed by bourgeois women,. He notes thus that while psychoanalysis was encouraging the wealthy neurotics to confess their incestuous impulses, a campaign was being waged in rural areas to suppress incest (129/171). The bourgeois family, having been subjected for over a century to a sexuality that incites incest, is now offered relief from the repression of incest. The poor, by contrast, only get suppression.

At a theoretical level, psychoanalysis asserts its universal applicability, but practically it is only offered as a treatment to an elite. The rest of the population by contrast is exposed to a psychological and psychiatric apparatus that does not take such close care of people's neuroses, though it is still decisively informed by psychoanalytic theory. This is not quite to say that Freud in any way intended to produce or reproduce such a social division through his methods. It is effectively rather an accidental interaction of his theories with class society. This would accord with Foucault's conception of the way power operates strategically. These are the 'specific class effects' sexuality has for different social strata (127/168).

Foucault claims that 'The history of the device of sexuality, as it has developed since the classical age, can serve as the archaeology of psychoanalysis' (130/172*). Psychoanalysis is thus the most recent phase in the history of sexuality for Foucault, the phase to which the repressive hypothesis decisively belongs. What we see with psychoanalysis is a new way of combining sexuality with alliance, displacing heredity and degenerescence, while serving the new function of differentiating classes within the device of sexuality. Foucault notes the coincidence of psychoanalysis and its theory of the Oedipus complex with the loss of paternal authority (130/172). In the nineteenth century, men had great legal power over their wives and children which they have since gradually lost. Foucault of course is implying that psychoanalysis has substituted for the loss of real power of the father, by establishing in its theories the father's place as ineluctable within the human psyche.

The repressive hypothesis developed from this tendency. Reich's theories are important to its development, according to Foucault (131/173). Where Reich thought we must overthrow capitalism to achieve sexuality, with a revolutionary intent, in fact his thought ended up captured within a power structure Reich did not see, the device of sexuality. Thus, says Foucault, the 'sexual "revolution"' envisaged by Reich was nothing of the kind: it was not revolutionary and did not require the abolition of capitalism or any other major change to the form of our society (131/172). Rather, it produced only 'a tactical displacement and reversal in the great device of sexuality' (131/172*). From Foucault's point of view it is sexuality itself that is the problem.

Despite the repressive hypothesis's political ambitions, I think we can moreover point to a certain snobbery inherent in the repressive hypothesis, particularly the form referred to by Foucault, which castigates working-class people for rejecting sexuality. That is, sexual liberation comes to be a marker of class and sophistication, and sexual reticence of an antiquated moralism. The repressive hypothesis thus comes to be another episode of the use of theories of repression to distinguish between classes.

Sexuality Now?

For Foucault then, the history of sexuality seems to culminate first in psychoanalysis, and then in the repressive hypothesis which it spawns but which outstrips and condemns it in turn.

I think it is noteworthy that, particularly outside France, something has appeared which is neither psychoanalysis, nor a psychoanalytic-inflected repressive hypothesis. In France, psychiatry and psychology remain largely dominated by psychoanalysis in its Lacanian inflexion, but this was a situation rather specific to France, as Foucault acknowledged at the time.[39] Particularly in the English-speaking countries, however, psychoanalysis has gone from being the dominant psychiatric modality to being a marginal and 'discredited' theory. This has not occurred, however, because of the repressive hypothesis in any recognisable form. Rather, psychoanalysis has been displaced by a psychology with a dual focus on the science of the brain and the science of genetics. In some ways, this is similar to nineteenth-century psychiatry, which also had the same ostensible interests in the neurological and hereditary. The great difference is that neurology and genetics have become unrecognisably more sophisticated since the nineteenth century.

This new science does not seem to have made any great difference to the device of sexuality, however. Empirically, our society seems as obsessed with sex as ever. The evolutionary perspective validates the importance of sex: sex is seen as an invariant biological imperative, as is the need to form families, hence a continued combination of sexuality with alliance. The threat of the biological notion of human sexuality is perhaps indicated in our increasingly panicked attitude toward sexual interactions between children and adults. These are mere suggestions, however: a full study would be necessary to extend Foucault's analysis in this way.

For his part, Foucault believed that things were moving if anything in an 'anti-sex' direction, that indicated by his own prescription (which we will examine below) towards pleasure.[40] He associates this tendency with a form of discourse in which sex is completely open, rather than hidden and then revealed. However, it would seem that there has been little movement in this direction, and that things are substantively as they were in the 1970s, notwithstanding some changes in the device of alliance (higher divorce rates, lower marriage rates, fewer children), which do not seem to have ended the general link of sex to alliance.

Biopower (Part Five, first half)

In Part Four of *The Will to Knowledge*, the chapters on power and the two on the history of sexuality have little linkage between them. These two themes, the conception of power and the history, come together, however, in Part Five.

Part Five is the densest and most involved of all the five parts of the book. It provides the conclusion to the book, and this conclusion has two moments to it, which I will deal with separately in detail.

Foucault begins Part Five with an account of the historical operation of power. This lasts ten pages in the English translation before a break in the text, after which Foucault explains how his history relates to sexuality, specifically in terms of what Foucault calls 'bio-power'. Foucault's use of this concept has been influential in a range of academic fields, and Part Five of *The Will to Knowledge* is the place where he primarily develops it. There then follows another break in the text, after which Foucault deals with what I call ontological questions about sex, that is, questions about how the power effects around sex relate to real things such as organs and bodies.

Sovereign Power

Foucault begins Part Five with a description of what we could call the traditional form of power, which he calls 'sovereign power'. This is power that refers to the 'sovereign', the one who rules over others, paradigmatically the king, or indeed the father. Foucault notes that this power traditionally implied the absolute power of life and death over the ruled. He notes that in the Roman family, the father was endowed with the right to kill the slaves he owned and even his children. This power thereafter diminished, such that sovereigns, either fathers or kings, have long lacked a right to kill their subjects at whim, though the trajectory between antiquity and the Middle Ages, where Foucault picks things up, is rather more complicated than this simplistic portrayal. In any case, during the medieval period, the rights of the sovereign were constrained within a framework of law. We have already seen how Foucault describes the historical valorisation of the law as a model of power since the Middle Ages in Chapter 1 of Part Four.

By this period, the right to kill had effectively been limited to a right to use lethal force in self-defence. 'Defence' here, however, could be construed quite broadly. On the one hand, it included a right of the king to wage war abroad that served merely to extend his power, since this in effect was necessary to build strength for defence. This right extended to the right to compel subjects to fight in wars, hence to risk their lives. It was then, as Foucault sees it, a right not only to kill but to expose others to the risk of death. Within the realm, the right to self-defence meant a right to punish the least insult with vicious brutality, since allowing people to insult the king invited a slippery slope to anarchy, against which the king's peace must be defended. Since all law refers to the authority of the king, all criminality is an affront to the king, and all but the pettiest kinds of criminality in the early modern period were liable to be punished by death. This was in effect a right of the sovereign to take revenge against anyone who breaks the law. This form of punishment, lethal and monarchical, is the object of a well-known florid description of an execution given by Foucault at the beginning of his previous book, *Discipline and Punish.*

In relation to the rights of the sovereign, Foucault refers here, in *The Will to Knowledge*, to the thought of seventeenth-century English philosopher Thomas Hobbes, whose best known work, *Leviathan*, is a justification of sovereign power. For Hobbes, we all have a natural right of limitless self-defence by extending our power, which leads to perpetual war. Everyone therefore, on Hobbes's account, gives up this right in exchange for peace, by transferring their rights to a sovereign, who then himself has this limitless right internationally, contending endlessly with other sovereigns and against internal threats. Foucault does not say whether he thinks Hobbes is right about the origin of sovereign power, mentioning also, in a footnote, the alternative view of the German philosopher Samuel von Pufendorf, a younger contemporary of Hobbes, which Foucault takes to have been that the sovereign's rights are something unlike those that existed before (135–6/178).

For Foucault, what is essential about this sovereign form of power is not its justification but its modus operandi, namely death. Though the sovereign's power was designated as 'the power of life and death', it was in fact, as Foucault puts it, a 'right to *make* die or *let* live' (136/178*).[41] That is, killing was the main way it exercised power on people – the nicest thing sovereign power did for its common subjects was to allow them to live without hurting them! In between these two alternatives, as we have seen, it could expose you to a risk of death without directly killing you. It is worth noting here the relative absence of what we take as the ordinary form of state coercion, imprisonment. As Foucault details in *Discipline and Punish*, until late modernity, surprising though it might seem to us, it was not a common punishment at all to lock someone away. To kill and to maim were the standard forms of punishment.

Foucault suggests thinking of this 'juridical form' (that is, form of legal procedure) as part of a broader societal form of power he calls 'deductive' (136/178). Medieval and early modern societies were governed in this way: the state existed solely though negative operations of subtraction vis-à-vis society. From the point of view of the state, society was treated as something extrinsic to it, effectively like a natural resource. The common people lived, worked, produced. The state simply took from them what it needed in the way of taxes; it did not intervene in society to produce anything. The only intervention that the sovereign made was to harm people to keep them in line, or to force them to serve him. Foucault calls this a right of 'taking' (*prise*): the sovereign takes someone's life, takes their money or takes hold of their body (136/179*).

Sovereign power has never gone away, according to Foucault. It has, however, ceased to be the primary form of political power, and this change in status has changed its operation significantly. Power has more generally shifted from a thoroughly negative form to become primarily productive, to produce more than destroy.

There is a paradox to this, however, which is that Foucault seems to suggest more people have been killed by politics than ever in this new era. It seems, indeed, though Foucault does not say as much, that we have more sovereign power, not less, today, even as the place of sovereign power within the overall operation of power in our society has declined. We have seen two phenomena since the nineteenth century unprecedented in history. We have seen wars in which tens of millions of people died in just a few years (the two world wars in the twentieth century being of course the prime examples). We have also seen 'holocausts', says Foucault, which of course refers primarily to the Holocaust, the genocide of millions of Jews by the Nazis during World War II, which Foucault takes here as exemplary of a number of such incidents of mega-slaughter.

I am dubious that the scale of deaths in these wars is in itself completely unprecedented. In the Thirty Years War in the seventeenth century in Germany, for example, at least a quarter of the entire population of Germany died – more than the reduction in population in Germany caused by World War II. Of course, this former war lasted five times as long as the latter one. Perhaps the decisive difference though is that the death in the two wars is of a different type. In the Thirty Years War, death was rife, but the result of indifference. Plague ran wild, people were malnourished, and soldiers looted and killed as they pleased. In World War II, by contrast, death was deliberate: the Holocaust was no accident, but rather centrally supervised, and conducted with military efficiency and industrial technology. The militarisation of populations into massive armies was genuinely unprecedented and the machinery of war produced at the time allowed direct killing on an industrial scale. Few Germans died from starvation during World War II, but entire cities were flattened by bombing.

This implies that technology is at the source of the difference, as indeed it is, but not only in the sense one might imagine. Certainly, the production of new technologies in the usual sense is crucial to this change: trains, machine guns, artillery, poison gas. However, Foucault's focus is on what he calls 'political technology' (145/191).

Where war is concerned, he posits a shift from war 'in the name of the sovereign' to war 'in the name of the existence of everyone' (137/180*). War ceased to be a matter essentially of a dispute between royal dynasties over territory, and became an existential struggle between nations. It was no longer sovereigns who warred, but entire populations, and this meant that the numbers of people involved, the extent to which they were involved, the desperation with which they fought, and the numbers killed increased commensurately. Though now for the first time governed by rules of war that ought to have prevented atrocities, wars in the twentieth century distinguish between civilians and combatants less than ever before. Much of this can be attributed to the emergence of new weapons that kill indiscriminately, aerial bombing being the key one, but at the same time the idea that wars are total, that it is an entire population versus another, has come into its own. Everyone in the nation is involved in the modern war effort in some way, given the economic unity of the nation, hence everyone becomes a target. For Foucault, the increase in destructive technology has driven this identification of population with war, finding its apogee in nuclear weapons, in which the entire population is for the first time literally threatened with annihilation (137/180). 'Massacres have become vital', as Foucault ironically puts it (137/180); vital then both in the sense of necessary to the functioning of power, and in the sense that people are killed in the name of safeguarding or of maximising life.

Clearly there is something paradoxical about this. For Foucault, this paradox is emblematised by the fact that at the same time that deaths in wars were increasing, the use of capital punishment was declining and indeed disappearing entirely. This latter change was because power was increasingly taking on the task of moving into people's lives and administering them. Once it does this, to kill people comes to be completely against the logic of power, since it destroys the very thing that is being administered.

The situation with capital punishment took an unexpected turn after *The Will to Knowledge* was written. At the time Foucault was writing, capital punishment had been suspended in the United States for several years as a result of a Supreme Court decision; however, it resumed from

1977. This does not necessarily imply that power shifted back decisively towards the use of death, however. Rather, capital punishment can be consistent with a power focused on making people live, as long as it serves that logic. Since capital punishment in the United States has been allowed to resume only as a punishment for murder, it takes the form of the ultimate defence of life.

So, suggests Foucault, 'we could say that the old right to *make* live or to *let* die is replaced by a power to *make* live or *expel* into death' (138/181*). Capital punishment is covered here as a form of 'expulsion'.

Even where capital punishment continues to be applied, moreover, it is in a form that is quite different to its early modern operation. Earlier, it was a bloody public spectacle, whereas it is today a relatively hidden, private, clean, medical procedure. Foucault refers to the more general fact that our society has more aversion to death than any before (138/181). Other cultures have lived in the presence of death, both animal and human, to a greater extent than ours can tolerate. Foucault thinks that this aversion to death owes less to some kind of 'new anxiety' about dying, than it does to a change in the form of power in our society. Previously, death was accorded great political significance, as the passage from earthly to heavenly sovereignty, hence 'the splendour that surrounded it was a matter of political ceremony' (138/182*). Nowadays, however, death is radically outside power, the one thing that cannot be incorporated into the public world, such that it becomes the supremely private moment. Previously, notes Foucault, suicide was an affront to sovereignty, either temporal or divine, thus illegal, because it implied a right to choose to die regardless of the will of the sovereign (139/182). Now, it is legalised, but becomes an object of intense study and hand-wringing, because as a rejection of life it is a rejection of everything we believe in, in effect. Suicide is now not only taboo because it is out of the control of sovereign power, but because it is a deliberate choice of death, and particularly because it is premature, wasteful, useless death, which does not serve but weakens the nation.

As Foucault points out, generally speaking, life and politics have been related for thousands of years. I think we could probably say something stronger in fact: neither power in Foucault's sense, nor politics, nor our history could have existed without the existence of biological life. What Foucault is referring to is not simply power over, or the politics of, life in some trivial sense. This relationship of power to life *simpliciter* he rather now names 'bio-history' (143/188). This is the first of three terms that

Foucault introduces here deriving from the Greek word for life, *bios*. Bio-history is not what he is interested in, however. Rather, he is interested in the specific effect, as yet unnamed, by which death has receded from life in recent centuries. He mentions here the greater health brought about by the agricultural revolution, which has made life longer for most people. This for Foucault created a larger space of life in which power could intervene, with biological existence for the first time becoming the theme of politics. It is not then that biological existence has entered politics for the first time, since the former always presupposed the latter to some extent. Rather, this is the first time politics has come to take biology to be its domain.

Anatomo-Politics and Biopolitics

Foucault says that a new 'power over life developed in two main forms', 'two poles' with a whole lot of 'intermediary relations' between them (139/182–3*). One form developed well before the other, and was initially not connected to power over life but only to sovereign power. This was a power over individual bodies in their mechanical capacities. Foucault calls it 'anatomo-politics' (deriving from the Greek *anatomia*, anatomy, literally meaning to cut apart), the politics of the body, instantiated in 'the *disciplines*' (139/183); he will also refer to it simply as 'discipline' (e.g. 140/184). The development of this disciplinary power was the general theme of *Discipline and Punish*, as indeed its title indicates. The second, newer pole focuses on what Foucault calls the 'species-body' (139/183). By this, he means that its focus is humans not as individuals but as a species, on our biology, which is not so much individual as interactive and reproductive. This pole he designates the '*bio-politics of the population*' (139/183). Between them, these two poles entail the control of life on both a large and a small scale.

The first pole comprises all kinds of disciplinary institutions in which bodies can be corralled and marshalled: medical (hospitals), pedagogical (schools, universities), economic (factories), punitive (prisons), military (barracks). Its historical origin was in the military, that is, simply in the service of sovereign power, by producing soldiers who could fight better by training their movements. The second form, biopolitics, sees the introduction of a range of forms of observation, primarily the collection of various kinds of statistics, and interventions to match, such as in health and the control of migration. The disciplinary institutions are indispensable to the monitoring, and even more so to the interventions, of biopolitics. For this reason, it indeed seems necessary that the introduction of anatomo-politics preceded that of biopolitics.

For Foucault, 'bio-politics' is 'what brings life and its mechanisms into the domain of explicit calculations and makes power-knowledge an agent of transformation of human life' (143/188*).[42] What is interesting about this is that it implies that previously power-knowledge was not an agent of transformation of human life, but rather human life got along, if not independently of power-knowledge, at least without being affected by power-knowledge in its very being. Foucault here refers this change to his earlier researches in *The Order of Things*, employing the signature concept of that book, the 'episteme', which refers to the basic rules for the ordering of knowledge in a particular era (143/189). In *The Order of Things*, Foucault had discovered certain widespread shifts at particular historical moments in the episteme of academic discourses concerned with studying humans. He now implies that one of these, the raising of the 'question of man' so important to his analysis in that earlier book, occurred because of the emergence of biopolitics. That is, the question of what we are as humans is not merely an academic question that emerged out of human curiosity, but correlative to the emergence of new ways of directing our behaviour in society.

Foucault argues that biopolitics was invented at a theoretical level before it was applied and thus linked up to discipline. He notes that there were in the eighteenth century discourses of discipline on the one hand (which he identifies with three French generals: Maurice de Saxe, the Comte de Guibert and Joseph Servan), and on the other discourses of biopolitics (Foucault lists here two Frenchmen, the economist François Quesnay and the demographer Jean-Baptiste Moheau, and a German demographer, Johann Peter Süssmilch). He then identifies 'Ideology' (understood in its oldest sense as literally the science of ideas, meaning a school whose primary representative was French thinker Destutt de Tracy, who was active at the beginning of the nineteenth century and tried to combine the study of economics with that of individual human faculties within a biology) as constituting a discursive bridge between the two poles, which emerged later than either and articulated a theoretical framework in which both society and the individual can be understood simultaneously (140/184).

Biopower

Foucault points out, however, that it was not the theoretical, but the concrete unity of the two 'techniques' that was decisive (140/184). This unity formed a single 'technology' (139/183), 'bio-power' (140/184). He claims that biopower was 'indispensable' to the development of capitalism (140–1/185). Both poles are implicated here. Discipline was necessary to create industrial production, a technique of control without which great factories could not have been run. Biopolitics was necessary to create the healthy workforce, and the 'accumulation' of workers (141/186). The techniques of biopower also allowed for the production of social stratification, that is, the separation of people into distinct social classes and groups. One's place in the hierarchy determined the techniques that were applied to you, and vice versa. Foucault has already given an example of this in his description of the application of sexuality variably to different classes.

'Bio-power' is not simply the mixture of life and power, but a power that takes life as its explicit target. This was not the case when power used death as its method: though it in a sense operated on life, since only living things can be killed, it did not take hold of life. Not that biopower takes hold of life entirely, Foucault is careful to note: life outstrips biopower constantly (143/188). Partly this is a reference to resistance, but it is also a reference to the non-existence of biopower for much of humanity, which is left in parts of the world, or substrata, which are outside of any power that maximises life.

Resistance to biopower has indeed been ubiquitous. It has not taken the form that might be expected, namely of a demand to return to a world of pure sovereign power. This resistance, emerging in the nineteenth century, also broke with the eschatology, the prediction of the end of the world, that had marked the earlier resistance to sovereign power (144–5/190). People did not want to go back to the relatively medieval forms of power, nor did they hope for religious salvation, for a messiah to lead them to a golden age. Rather, resistance to biopower itself appears as a form of politics of life. Though these struggles were often expressed in the juridical-legal language of rights, the content of the demands made were biological: people demanded the right to life, to their body, to health. Thus, political struggles continue to this day to be demands not for the abolition of biopower, but for rights, for inclusion in the protections and benefits of biopower.

The rights now demanded would not, Foucault thinks, have made sense in the old order. Although the discourse of rights is used, the old model of the law has lost its prominence. A new model, that of the norm, has risen with biopower as a model to partially replace the law

(144/189). The law is bound to enforcement, that is, to the politics of death. Biopower, by contrast, is not concerned simply to separate the licit from the illicit (it leaves that job to the law and, by extension, to sovereign power). Rather, it involves much more complex forms of graded measurement. It needs to, indeed, because its remit is not to decide who will live and who will die, but to transform life in multifarious ways. This means it is not a matter of creating binary divisions, of saying yes or no, but rather establishes various norms around which it can be decided what is normal and abnormal, with a continuous gradation of cases between the two. The law, says Foucault, is brought into this process: it comes itself to operate as a norm.

Still, the emergence of biopower from the end of the eighteenth century has not abolished sovereign power, but simply overshadowed it. Rather, power has now acquired a dual nature: on the one hand, subtracting, violent and repressive, and on the other, the nurturing welfare state.

What is crucial here is the emergence of the population itself. In the earlier deductive form of power, there were only people, whose existence, though of vital importance to the sovereign, was of no great concern for the sovereign beyond his need to take from them, unless they disobeyed him, in which case he killed them. Before biopolitics, there is no population, just people in a territory. In English (though of course Foucault does not note this), the word population, to mean the people who live in a place, only came into use in the seventeenth century. The emergence of the population is what makes possible forms of national solidarity that lead populations as such to fight one another, and thus to total war. Sovereign power is harnessed to biopower to produce something more terrible than sovereign power itself could have managed. In a period in which the killing of citizens by the state has been largely done away with, to kill people outside the nation has remained relatively unproblematic for the nation state, since it is not concerned with administering such persons. Moreover, once the state's business comes to be keeping its citizens alive, the survival of citizens is linked to the well-being of the state, such that the lives of citizens can be risked in wars to protect the state – after all, the lives that are risked in furthering the nation's interests would be put at risk effectively by failing to secure this national interest. Still, this risking of lives of citizens is basically just the continuation of what happened already under sovereign power – it is in effect the continuation of the older sovereign form, even if it now has an additional, biopolitical complexion.

The History of Biopower

Foucault says little in *The Will to Knowledge* about where biopower comes from and despite later giving a set of lectures called *The Birth of Biopolitics*, these contain very little to live up to their title, as Foucault himself acknowledges within them, but in work immediately afterwards he extends his analysis to the Christian period, finding in Christianity a distinct form of power that he calls 'pastoral power'.[43] This power comes originally from Eastern cultures, particularly the Jews, and enters Europe through Christianity. Unlike Western political culture, which is focused on territorial dominion, pastoral power follows the model of a shepherd and his flock, with a ruler being concerned about the individual well-being of subjects. In Europe, for a millennium, there was a divide between a political power that was indifferent to the well-being of its subjects, and the Church which, influenced by the Eastern attitudes embedded in Christianity, ministered to people on a relatively caring and individual basis. Biopower thus represents the appropriation of the functions of the Church by the secular state, though of course with different, more worldly concerns. This applies to both biopolitics and discipline. Biopolitics originated in the Church's concern with the well-being of the flock, while discipline originated in the intense routinisation of life in monastic institutions.

Biopower and Sex

Foucault claims that it is biopower that explains the importance that sexuality has taken on in recent centuries. Sex is for Foucault the 'hinge between the two axes' of biopower, discipline and biopolitics (145/191*), where the control of the individual body connects up to the regulation of the population. The two connect here primarily because sex is the thing you do with your body that produces new human beings, hence is an act between two persons (paradigmatically) that is absolutely vital to the population. It is also important from a biopolitical perspective, in a somewhat opposite direction, as a major vector for the transmission of disease. It is moreover an important social relation in its own right from the political point of view, once the social importance of the device of alliance is taken into account. However, once in existence, sexuality has come into its own as a form of control that exceeds these anchors: the categorisation of people according to perversions and the concern about perversions outstripped any simple concern about reproduction and disease, to operate rather as a grid for a social control that combined concerns about the regulation of population with the need to mark and control individuals.

Foucault points out that each of 'the four great lines of attack' of the 'politics of sex' over the last two centuries – the sexualisation of children, hysterisation of women, psychiatrisation of perversions, and socialisation of procreation – reflects this combination of discipline and biopolitics (146/193). With women and children, the application was disciplinary, to get them to conform, but ultimately served biopolitical ends in terms of the health of society. With birth control, the aim was immediately biopolitical, to alter the rate of demographic change across the population, but the means disciplinary, applied necessarily to individual bodies (147/193).

Foucault returns to the theme of blood here, linking its importance in the device of alliance to sovereign power: our societies were previously obsessed with blood, with spilling it, with preserving it (147/194). For Foucault, sex replaces blood here as the principle of our society. Blood was, says Foucault, '*a reality with a symbolic function*' (147/194). This means it is something real, that exists regardless of whether or not it plays this crucial role in power, but it contingently took on a certain 'symbolic function', that is, a function within a regime of power-knowledge. Sexuality, on the other hand, Foucault calls '*an effect with a meaning-value*' (147/195). By classifying sexuality as an effect rather than a reality, I think Foucault means to imply that sexuality is less real than blood, since an effect is dependent on its cause – just how real he thinks it is, we will see below. What is the difference moreover between a symbolic function and a 'meaning-value'? Well, blood was something that operated as a symbol of something else, functioning to represent that thing in discourse. It was not literally blood, the red stuff in the circulatory system, that preoccupied the medieval mind, so much as the thing it stood for, familial connections. By contrast, sexuality is seen as having value, as being valuable and meaningful in itself. Sexuality is thus simultaneously less real but much more important in the economy of power-knowledge than blood used to be.

Foucault is careful to note that we should not see this shift from blood to sex as the main change that ushered in modernity (148/195). He is clear rather that he is focusing on this because he is writing a history of sexuality. From a more general point of view, it is the shift in forms of power, the establishment of biopower, that is more important.

Just as biopower did not erase what existed before, so too the shift from blood to sexuality was not absolute. Rather, blood was still invoked. The first case of this Foucault details is de Sade's writing, which he already discussed earlier in the book. De Sade's work is notorious for its mixture of descriptions of sexual excess with descriptions of blood-letting. Foucault sees this as important, with de Sade's version of sex not involving norms, only sovereignty (149/196). It would seem then that de Sade represents a crossover that harks back to an older thematics of blood.

The more important case Foucault discusses, however, is eugenics (the selective breeding of human beings) and racism. He develops this discussion further in *Society Must Be Defended*, which is in effect a geneal-ogy of racism, and also includes a more detailed treatment of biopower than that found in *The Will to Knowledge*. The role of blood as a theme in eugenics and racism is self-evident: these are modern scientific versions of the older obsession with heredity and breeding. Rather than merely concern itself with the heredity and breeding of the elite, however, eugenics is a discourse that is biopolitical, concerned with the breeding of an entire population. In effect, eugenics merely logically extends the basic biopolitical concern with the health of the population in general. Racism does something more, however, understanding the population itself as an entity based on blood, which has blood in common, extend-ing the notion of blood as a tie of family found in the device of alliance to the level of demography.

Eugenics and racism have both become taboo in recent decades, but from the late nineteenth century to the mid-twentieth century the prac-tice of eugenics and discourse of racism were taken up to some extent by most governments. In the absence of the kind of sophisticated knowl-edge of genetics that we have today, eugenics at that time was based on a racist pseudo-science, on a theory of the superiority of certain races and the pureness of blood stock based in the older thematic of blood, but mobilising a more modern biologistic, often pseudo-Darwinian concep-tual framework, seeing races of humans in effect as competing species.

The apogee of this tendency was Nazism. Foucault aptly describes Nazism as both 'the most naïve and the most cunning' form of such discourse (149/197*). It is naïve, I take it, because its basic presupposi-tions regarding race, Aryan purity versus the pollution of race-mixing, were both utterly simple and complete nonsense (there never was any pure Aryan race, nor any evidence that there was one; there was never any evidence either that race-mixing is deleterious or dangerous).

However, what it built on this stupid foundation was quite sophisticated: an efficient racist state apparatus, and a large body of scientific research. Nazism represented an extreme form of totalitarian society too, of course, what Foucault here calls *étatisation*, a French phrase normally used to refer to nationalisation, but which clearly indicates the growth in the power of the state (*État*), hence Hurley's translation of it as 'state control' (150/197). Eugenics and racism call for this growth in the power of the state, by requiring the extensive investigation of our identities and intimate regulation of our breeding.

Foucault complains that history has reduced the sexual side of Nazism to something laughable while according Nazi blood myths the status of the cause of the greatest massacre in memory (150/197). I take it his point here is that in fact the sexual side of Nazi policies, if not directly the cause of the slaughter, was nevertheless not a minor or accidental element in the Nazi philosophy or state.

For Foucault, the main opposite tendency to eugenic racism was psychoanalysis, which tries to make sexuality a matter of law (150/197–8). This has already been discussed in relation to the device of alliance in his genealogy of sexuality. While psychoanalysis is here to be lauded for opposing racism, Foucault's point is that both law and blood are old models that link sexuality to traditional forms of power, and as such are both politically conservative and theoretically inadequate.

Appropriations of Foucault's Concepts

Foucault did not in fact invent the concept of biopolitics, but he did introduce it into the theoretical humanities and social sciences, and indeed there is no evidence that Foucault's use of the term owes anything to any previous use.[44]

While many scholars have used Foucault's concept, some prominent thinkers have developed original conceptions of biopolitics with explicit references to Foucault's work, which indeed diverge from Foucault more than they seem to realise. The result is that many competing senses of the term circulate in the current humanities and social science literature. For the sake of clarity as to what Foucault is talking about, I will briefly explain the differences here.

Agamben

Firstly, the Italian philosopher Giorgio Agamben has developed his own conception of 'biopolitics' (though he does not use the word 'biopower'), initially and most famously in his *Homo Sacer*. For Agamben, 'biopolitics' means any politics that takes life as its target. This is, I think, quite simply any politics that has existed in history; Agamben's biopolitics is coextensive with Foucault's bio-history. Certainly, Agamben thinks biopolitics has existed at least since ancient Greece. Agamben also takes biopolitics to mean more or less the same thing as 'sovereign power', running these two quite different notions of Foucault's into one, ubiquitous form of power.

Hardt and Negri

Two neo-Marxists, the Italian philosopher Antonio Negri and an American, Michael Hardt, collaboratively wrote an extraordinarily popular book, *Empire*, which has since spawned two sequels, in which they take up Foucault's terms 'bio-power' and 'bio-politics'. Their uses, however, have very little to do with Foucault's. They take biopower and biopolitics as polar opposites, according to a long-standing distinction in Negri's work between 'constituted' and 'constitutive' power. Hardt and Negri see the world as divided between a globalised form of network power, 'Empire', and a general global power of the people who are subjugated by it, but also from whom it draws its power, the 'multitude'. This is somewhat redolent of Foucault's distinction between power and resistance, but, as we have seen above, the idea of a power which has no inventive impetus of its own is precisely a form of traditional Marxist conception of power that he rejects. Hardt and Negri use 'biopolitics' to refer to the constitutive power of the multitude, and 'biopower' to refer to the constituted power of Empire. As such, for them, these terms refer to something that is perhaps a few decades old, rather than centuries old as in Foucault's use of the terms.

Later Developments

Governmentality

While other thinkers have continued to take up Foucault's notion of biopolitics decades after he formulated it, he himself stopped using it almost entirely and almost immediately. After *The Will to Knowledge*, he scarcely mentions it. It appears prominently in the title of his 1979 lectures *The Birth of Biopolitics*, but hardly at all inside, and then only by way of apology that he is not in fact talking about biopolitics as he had intended to. What he talks about here instead is a different concept, one he invented, 'governmentality', which has itself been immensely influential after Foucault. We have already mentioned this in relation to power above.

Governmentality seems at points simply to replace 'bio-politics' for Foucault; where he had spoken of sovereign power, discipline and biopolitics, he now groups 'sovereignty, discipline and governmental management'.[45] The question for us is whether this means that Foucault thought there was some problem with the notion of biopower and biopolitics, such that he had to dispense with them. We should first note that he certainly never actually renounced them, so if such a problem did exist, he did not acknowledge it explicitly, and that the replacement occurs only in lecture series he never had published, whereas *The Will to Knowledge* is Foucault's decisive published output of the late 1970s. The dropping of the 'bio-' terminology is moreover not total, inasmuch as there are scattered uses of it in his later work, albeit only minor ones made in passing.

Biopower Today

It certainly does not seem to me that there has been any change in contemporary politics that might have motivated Foucault to drop these notions. Paul Rabinow and Nikolas Rose, though they do not suggest this as the reason for Foucault's shift in terminology, do suggest that sexuality is possibly declining as the point of anatomo-politics–biopolitics nexus.[46] I think that there is no substance to this claim, either in terms of empirical changes to the apparatus or in the field of sexuality itself. Certainly, there have been many changes, but the idea that either the combination of anatomo-politics and biopolitics or our society's obsession with sex(uality) has declined seems to me to be simply baseless.

Something that has happened since Foucault wrote was the decline of mass death in wars. Or, more accurately, a decline in the instance of mass deaths among troops from First World countries in wars. Wars continue to kill millions of people in the Third World, whether they are wars waged by the First World against the Third, or within the Third World. It seems, however, that the most 'advanced' countries are unwilling to risk the lives of their citizens as they used to. Does this indicate a decline in sovereign power vis-à-vis biopower?

There has been some variation in this effect, most markedly seen in the war against Iraq in 1990–1, when tens of thousands of Iraqis were killed, while most casualties on the other side, that of the USA and its allies, resulted from accidents. The wars of the last decade, most noticeably the invasion of Iraq in 2003, have resulted in more risk to Western soldiers, but the disparity between numbers of natives versus numbers of invaders killed is enormous. There is still much less risk of death involved for 'our' troops than for example in the much more brutal Vietnam War three decades previously. The interpretation I would offer here is simple, and entirely within Foucault's framework. Technological developments have lessened the risk of death somewhat, but there is also less of a justification in biopolitical terms for a risk of death. In the world wars, the survival of populations was supposedly at risk. This also seemed to be the case in the Cold War climate in which Vietnam was invaded. However, the wars against Iraq were prosecuted merely in the name of strategic interests and the freedom of other peoples, not the very existence of our own population. Clearly there was some feeling of existential threat to the USA after September 11, and the level of casualties tolerated in its wars increased concomitantly.

The Ontology of Sex (Part Five, second half)

After his analysis of biopower, Foucault moves, in the final ten or so pages of the English translation, onto what I refer to as the ontology of sex. By this, I mean the deceptively simple question, 'What is sex?' He also considers here the question of what can be done to resist the device of sex as he has described it. In this section then, I look at the philosophical underpinnings of Foucault's position, how he thinks the historical 'construction' of sexuality, and how he relates to the ostensibly 'real' factors of human bodies, pleasures and desire.

Foucault begins this section of his book by once again imagining an objection to his position. This time, it is not an objection to his specific historical claims, but to the overall 'historicism' of his perspective. That is to say, it may be objected that Foucault's fixation with history causes him to miss the elephant in the room, which is sexuality itself. Rather, it might be said that one needs to uncover sexuality through psychology and physiology, not an inquiry into the way it has historically been discussed, which after all is rather a history of failures at understanding sexuality. At the very least, it might be argued that one cannot do the history of sexuality independently from saying what sexuality itself is, but Foucault seems to have made almost no attempt to define this object. He rather speaks as if sexuality is just a historical invention. Specifically, he anticipates the objection that he has ignored the reality of sex itself, the sexual act, that he instead talks about the discourse of 'sexuality as if sex did not exist' (151/199).

The implicit assumption behind this objection is that, whereas sexuality may be taken to be something cultural, and thus historically variable, hence something about which a history of discourses will tell us much, this sexuality revolves around sex itself, a natural thing that people have always engaged in, which is based in our fundamental biological nature and hence is real and essentially invariant. While there may be some variation in the way people practise sex over the centuries, the basic 'facts of life' might be said to remain the same. The guiding thought of this objection then is that sexuality is something that has been constructed around and distorts sex. Foucault tells us in an interview that this was his own initial thinking about the topic before researching the book.[47]

The objection Foucault imagines here allows that all he has said so far in the book is true, but that it is inadequate as a treatment of sexuality because historical discourses can only be fully understood in relation to the thing they discuss, in this case sex itself. While this objection allows that an older approach to sexuality that reads everything about sexuality as emanating from biological sex is also wrong, it insists that Foucault goes too far in the opposite direction. It ends with a barb, an accusation that Foucault has 'castrated' sexuality by leaving out biological sex (151/200).

Foucault's initial defence to this objection is to say that to talk about sexuality without reference to biology does not imply a rejection of biological facts or their importance. His earlier 'archaeological' studies of the 1960s of course were works that precisely studied discourses without much concern for the reality of their objects. Moreover, he points out, in this text he has not shied away from concrete reality in the way that he used to. He has in particular mentioned the body continually: for him one point of what he has been saying is to deal with the connection of power to the body. That is, for him the point is to show how history (which seems here to be synonymous with power, or at least the history of power) and biology affect one another (152/200). What he is doing then, as he puts it, is not to do a 'history of mentalities', which is to say, a history of the way people thought about or related to things, but rather a 'history of bodies', showing what has happened at a material level.

It is not immediately obvious that Foucault has actually done this, however. It is certainly true that he has talked about bodies a lot. He has talked about discourses that are about bodies, and about the way bodies are affected by discourses, and how entire technologies of power involving discourses grasp bodies. But has he actually effectively linked what he has said back to the body, or has he rather remained at the level of discourse? Discourse is not a mere mentality, a thing inside people's heads, but rather a matter of concrete, public discursive acts. It is not directly physical in the way that a body is, however. Yet, I do think Foucault manages to produce a materialist account of sexuality, but this is not so much to be found in his initial historical discussion, for all its invocation of bodies, but in the political discussion later in the book that explains sexuality in terms of the convergence of political strategies, technologies and devices based on real effects, on the production of lives and bodies, on controlling and transforming them. Talking about *The Will to Knowledge* immediately after its publication, Foucault says:

> What I want to show is how power relations can materially penetrate the body in depth, without depending even on the mediation of the subject's own representations. If power takes hold on the body, this isn't through its having first to be interiorised in people's consciousnesses. There is a network or circuit of bio-power, or somato-power, which acts as the formative matrix of sexuality itself as the historical and cultural phenomenon within which we seem at once to recognise and lose ourselves.[48]

Neither the person being subjected then, nor the person subjecting them, has to think about the process of subjection for it to take place. No one in the system has to think about what is really happening at the level of power for it to happen. The investment of the body in relation to sexuality is thus a matter of biopower controlling us through sex, even without us necessarily realising it.

Still, suggests Foucault, it might be objected that while he is happy enough to bring bodies into his account, sex itself is excluded. If it is the body that power attaches to and transforms here, is sex not the specific part or the activity of the body that sexuality attaches to?

Foucault is dubious about the very notion of 'sex', however. He questions whether sex exists objectively in itself as a reality, or whether it is not an idea 'formed across the different strategies of power' (152/202*). He claims that during the development of the device of sexuality, 'sex' came to be posited as a thing in its own right not identifiable with particular parts or sensations of the body (152–3/201). He then goes on to discuss it in relation to each of the four great strategies of sexuality. In relation to women, 'sex' was defined in three ways: as what women and men have in common (that is, presumably, that they both have a sex, female in the first case, male in the second, though it might also mean that they have sexual intercourse together, or indeed from a psychoanalytic point of view that the woman desires the man's *sexe*, his penis); as the thing that belongs to women (who used to be referred to as 'the sex' for this reason; the distinction between men and women marks women as different to masculinity, which is the default, normal sex); and as the thing that constitutes the woman's body itself (here it could be a reference to either femaleness or to genitalia or both). Sex was both the positive principle of hysteria, in the sense that it was caused by femaleness, and the thing the lack of which (sexual intercourse, the penis) caused it. Somewhat similarly, children were also defined as both having (anatomically) and lacking (reproductively) sex, while of course their behaviour saw it both evidenced and banned. In the case of perversion, the problem was the attachment of the sexual instinct to fetishised objects. When it came to procreation, the problem was the divergence of sexual pleasure from the procreative function. In both of these two last cases, sex did something again that it was not supposed to, led to behaviours other than those it was supposed to.

What all of this means, says Foucault, is that, across all of these strategies, a certain concept of sex was developed that groups together many different kinds of things 'in an artificial unity', comprising 'anatomical elements, biological functions, conducts, sensations, and pleasures' (154/204). Sex then artificially brings together various real things under its single umbrella, for essentially political reasons. This 'fictitious unity' could then be produced as an explanation for anything and everything, and of course could be discovered anywhere, given how diverse the things it brought together were, meaning it obtains unique importance as a 'signifier' (in effect, as a word). What was done was to seize on some biological facts – presumably ones such as that some diseases are hereditary, that there are some biological differences between men and women and children and adults – and use these as a 'guarantee of the quasi-scientificity' (that is, a guarantee makes the discourse of sexuality appear scientific), and at the same time as 'a principle of normality' (155/204). It is interesting that this constitutes a kind of contradiction, even though it might not be immediately apparent that it does. We are used to using biology as a source of norms, even though it is strictly speaking not possible to deduce the values from scientific facts. We are used to positing a 'natural' biological functioning of humans and then imposing this as a norm for our behaviour. Things that are 'unnatural' are understood to be bad, either in the sense of a medical disorder or a moral failing, even though nothing that exists can be truly unnatural from a scientific point of view. Homosexuality for a long time was seen in this light, as a behaviour that violated the laws of biology. Today, I would think suspicion is more likely to fall on celibacy. It is not a criminal behaviour as homosexuality once was, but certainly is seen as an unnatural aberration requiring intervention of some kind.

So, the creation of a single category that includes the penis, procreation, the difference between men and women, and the pleasure of one body touching another is for Foucault an artificial category uniquely found in our culture. This series of course seems obvious to us, indeed natural, but this is to be expected since being part of our sexual culture means precisely seeing sex as a natural, biological reality. It is this, as Foucault notes, that is the basis of the repressive hypothesis's view of sex is a stubborn biological reality that tries to express itself and has to be held down.

Sex, however, is not a natural object like our heart or lungs that exists as such whether we name it or not. Rather, it is something that groups together diverse things in a heterogeneous category, altering them through the process of grouping them: parts of the body, pleasures, words, desires, all of which exist in themselves regardless of the existence of the device of sexuality, are changed in various ways by being imbricated in it. There are then natural things that are shaped by power, but sex is not such a thing. It is not nature that is the basis of the notion of 'sex' for Foucault; if anything, it is biopower that is its underlying principle.

Far from being the reality that power seizes then, Foucault concludes that sex is 'the most speculative, most ideal, and most internal in a device of sexuality organised by power' (155/205*). Nevertheless, sex is perceived as essential, not only to sexuality, but to human being. Dwelling inside the device of sexuality, we can only understand ourselves, our bodies, our identities, through sex. Now, sex seems the most important thing in the world for us, 'more important than our soul, more important almost than our life': 'sex is worth dying for' (156/206). We can of course link these claims to the notion that in biopower the service of life may require an exposure to the risk of death.

This constitutes a massive reversal of the situation during the

Christian period, in which bodies were viewed with dread suspicion. It represents also a replacement of the valuation of love with a valuation of sex. Sex is, in short, 'desirable' (156/207). This seems like something of an understatement after Foucault's comment that sex is worth dying for, to suggest that it is just something we like. However, the French *désirable* specifically connotes that something is sexually desirable. Foucault's point then is that the very artificial category of sex arouses a specifically sexual desire in us, in the sense that we feel aroused by sex, by this fictitious object, by the idea, the word.

Foucault now quotes twice in one page from the works of English writer D. H. Lawrence (157/207–8). The first quotation is identified by Foucault as coming from Lawrence's novel *The Plumed Serpent*. The second quotation is not identified, but is from an essay Lawrence wrote about his best-known novel, *Lady Chatterley's Lover*, entitled 'A propos of *Lady Chatterley's Lover*'. That novel had gained great notoriety for its sexually explicit content, and was effectively banned in Britain for more than thirty years. In this essay that Foucault quotes from, Lawrence responds to the censorship of the work. Lawrence argues that humans have 'evolved' beyond the need for censorship, and that we are so civilised that thinking about sex clearly and honestly now will in fact lead us not to engage in sexual debauchery, but to chastity. In this, Lawrence's position clearly resembles that behind the sex education Foucault discusses earlier in his book. The 'conscious realization of sex' that Foucault quotes Lawrence talking about here is supposed to be a realisation of sex in consciousness itself, divorced from any physical activity. Lawrence goes on to rail against permissive, libertine attitudes to sex, since these do not show the proper awe of sex, before claiming that everything today is 'counterfeit' and we need to re-establish 'real' sex and love. Lawrence is not putting forward the repressive hypothesis then, since he holds that the development of self-control is required for sexual liberation, and thus seems to favour repression of a certain type, but is close to the repressive hypothesis, and certainly employing common tropes found in discourses of sexuality: sex is incredibly important, and there is a secret of sex which must be revealed.

Foucault suggests that one day all such thinking might seem strange. His point is that these ideas are peculiar to our society. Only our society has produced this notion of 'sex', and therefore only our society can have been concerned with its truth, whether by opposition to repression or through sublimation of base desires. Our obsession with sex

Foucault thinks can be imagined as rather funny from a standpoint outside our culture, particularly when one considers how we both continually produce sex and then reprimand ourselves for not realising it fully enough.

He refers to the 'reproach of pansexualism' raised against psychoanalysis (158/209). 'Pansexualism' would be to connect everything to, or indeed reduce everything down to, sexual drives. Foucault thinks that these objections will seem ridiculous from a future perspective, since the objections came from a quarter that was morally scandalised by the frank approach to sexuality of psychoanalysis, but conversely that psychoanalysis's dismissal of this reproach as mere prudishness will be seen as even more ridiculous, that in effect it is psychoanalysis's position that will seem most ridiculous. Presumably for Foucault this is because psychoanalysis asks no critical question about the concept of sex, where it comes from, or what its function is. Indeed, according to him, psychoanalysts (therefore) congratulated themselves for discovering the ubiquity of sex, when they were really standing in the long line of its production (159/210). Here, Foucault is not far from Deleuze and Guattari's critique of psychoanalysis.

Bodies and Pleasures

Here, Foucault's book ends. There is, however, a paragraph in the final pages, easily missed, perhaps, between the two quotes from Lawrence, in the middle of page 157 in the English translation, that is so important that we must pay it special attention. Most of this paragraph recapitulates what Foucault has said already: it is not sex that is real and sexuality that is ideal. He goes further here, however, and indicates that, if anything, it is the other way round: sexuality is 'very real' as a historical formation, whereas sex is merely a 'speculative element' involved in sexuality (157/207).

Deleuze interprets Foucault here as saying that sexuality is in fact something that exists throughout history, which this artificial thing called sex then pins down.[49] This is not Foucault's thesis here, although it does seem to have been his view circa 1970.[50] This is what I would expect in light of my view that the repressive hypothesis is Foucault's own earlier position, since the view that sexuality is transcendent is essential to the repressive hypothesis. In *The Will to Knowledge*, however, Foucault's thesis is that sexuality is a historical device that produces sex as its particular object. That this historical device is real does not imply that it exists transcendentally. Sexuality only exists in late modernity, therefore. Indeed, the second and third volumes of *The History of Sexuality*, despite the title, do not technically deal with sexuality per se, though they deal with things that today are defined as 'sexual'.

It is the end of the paragraph that is the most interesting part, in that it is the only point of the book where Foucault suggests some kind of practical implication of his analysis. Here, he concludes, unsurprisingly enough, that 'saying yes to sex' in effect also means to say yes to power (157/208–9). This does not logically imply that we can say no to power whenever we say no to sex, just that saying yes to sex is not an avenue of resistance as the repressive hypothesis indicates. Rather than simply advising us to 'say no to sex', Foucault advocates a 'tactical reversal of the diverse mechanisms of sexuality . . . against the holds of power' (157/208*). To resist power, he says we should instead assert (the phrase he uses is to *faire valoir* – literally to 'make valuable') 'bodies, pleasures, and knowledges, in their multiplicity and their possibility of resistance'.

He is saying that in our bodies, in our pleasures and even our knowledges there are potentials to resist. Now, this is vague advice, and presumably deliberately so. Foucault would seem to be reticent enough about giving any advice at all. He does not say anything to specify what the potentials here are. What he does do in the next sentence is distinguish between 'bodies and pleasures' on the one hand and 'sex-desire' on the other. This is interesting, because it apparently puts desire on the side of sex, this fictional unity, and of power, rather than on the side of bodies and pleasures, real and relatively resistant.

I am far from alone in assigning peculiar importance to these sentences. Ladelle McWhorter wrote an entire book, entitled *Bodies and Pleasures*, in which she detailed her autobiographical attempt to think through and practise the second of these sentences, or, indeed, perhaps only its last phrase. It is undoubtedly a mark of how little practical advice Foucault gives us that this tiny kernel of advice for resistance should have been seized on to such an extent.

The interpretation I had of this passage on first reading it (and its importance was immediately manifest) was that it implied we could resist sex by attending to our bodies and the pleasures we feel, focusing on these rather than on the concepts that were imposed on them. I am quite sure now that this interpretation was wrong. We cannot really have non-conceptual practices, I would argue, and certainly Foucault does not think we can.[51] This is why in the penultimate sentence of the paragraph he mentions 'knowledges' together with bodies and pleasures. We cannot just retreat to pure physicality against sex and sexuality. If Foucault meant that, he would simply be repeating the repressive hypothesis, in the form of saying that pleasures and bodies are a natural reality that has been repressed by sex-desire and needs to be liberated. He in fact specifically imputes such a view to the repressive hypothesis: in his description of it at the beginning of the book, he includes amongst its aims 'a restoration of pleasure within the real' (5/12*). This then is not what he is advocating himself. He is not claiming that we can liberate bodies and pleasures.

Here, Hurley's translation has I think caused some problems, though not through any serious inaccuracy and not in a way that Hurley could have anticipated. Hurley has Foucault saying that bodies and pleasures should be 'the rallying point for the counterattack against' sexuality. Foucault does not say 'rallying point', however, but *point d'appui*. Clearly there is a 'point' here but this point is one of *appui*, 'support'. So Foucault says bodies and pleasures are a point of support; this phrase *point d'appui* is usually translated into English as 'fulcrum'. A fulcrum is the point at which a lever pivots. That is bodies and pleasures are not seen as something to rally towards by Foucault, but to pivot off, as a base, a springboard. Another translation into English would be as foundation. Now, to be fair to Hurley, *point d'appui* has a military meaning, and in this context it could be translated as 'rallying point', that is, the place that troops base themselves and go back to. The phrase 'point d'appui' is indeed used untranslated within English military terminology in this way. Given Foucault's propensity to use military vocabulary, this translation seems reasonable. The problem is that I think 'rallying point' is apt to mislead, because it implies something we rally towards. The military point d'appui is something rallied towards only in order to form up and then carry forth against the foe. This is why the French refer to such a place as a 'point of support', a place that one can go to if needed in order to carry on thereafter, with the subsequent operation, not the rallying, being the main thing.

Thus, the point about bodies and pleasures is that they are things we can appeal to in the construction of new knowledges and power relations, and indeed a transformation of bodies and pleasures themselves. It is certainly not that Foucault thinks either pleasure or bodies are intrinsically against power – he clearly thinks that sexuality has pleasure as a support, and has invested bodies. The question here is what then distinguishes pleasures and bodies from desire, why Foucault places desire on the other side.

The point of Foucault's notion of 'sex-desire' (used uniquely here in this one passage at the end of the book) is that desire is so tied to sex that it is not possible to use desire against sex. The problem with this position of Foucault's, it seems to me, is that the same thing can be said of pleasure. What we find pleasurable or not is hardly independent from sex: it changes our pleasure as it changes our desire. Indeed, Foucault allows earlier in the book that pleasure and bodies and knowledges are all deeply affected by sexuality.

Foucault does not really explain his reasoning here, but provides many explanations in interviews afterwards when questioned.

One explanation, given in a 1978 interview – albeit an interview that, unusually, he had not edited for publication – is that it is desire, not pleasure that is used by the medical establishment to determine the abnormality of pleasures.[52] This goes back to Christianity, for Foucault, where desire rather than pleasure was at stake in sin. He thus allows that pleasure is seized and categorised as abnormal within the device of sexuality, but that desire is somehow closer to power as the point by which power grasps pleasure. As Foucault points out here and elsewhere, in Catholicism and psychoanalysis, it is desire that is primarily at stake.[53]

Here, I think Foucault's failure to deal with the specificity of the post-psychoanalytic situation found in English-speaking psychiatry and psychology, already discussed above, is problematic. It is perhaps true that even English-speaking psychiatrists talk about desire more than pleasure. However, since behaviourism, the accent in English-language psychology has been not on intentions, but on acts. What is taken to be abnormal is not so much having desires, but in acting. If one merely desires, or takes pleasure in thoughts, rather than acts, there is no diagnosable pathology. It does not therefore seem to me that desire is significantly more implicated in contemporary psychology or psychiatry in the Anglosphere than pleasure. It seems to me moreover that the repressive hypothesis is at least as concerned with liberating pleasure as with liberating desire.

What is at stake here can be made clearer by looking at the key example of homosexuality. As I have said above, sexuality today perhaps even primarily refers to the homo-/heterosexuality distinction. This distinction is made primarily on the basis of what one desires, whether one desires people of the same sex or the other sex, it is true. But I do not think that it excludes what one takes pleasure in or what acts one engages in with one's body. The sex of the people whose contact gives us pleasure, the sex of the people we have intercourse with, are both clearly used to judge our sexuality.

Foucault claims pleasure is an empty concept that can have new meanings applied to it, that it is not caught up in discourses like the repressive hypothesis in the way that desire is.[54] This strikes me as dubious, inasmuch as ordinary people's attachment to sex as important certainly involves the valorisation of particular pleasures along with the valorisation of desire. Pleasures can be categorised sexually just as much as desire can be. It would be wrong to suggest, I think, that we experience a touch simply as pleasure regardless of who is touching us, regardless of what sex they are, for example. Moreover, it does not seem to me that bodies are immune from the machinations of sex. Bodies themselves are categorised as sexually normal and abnormal in themselves. The body of an intersex person is I think, lamentably, itself generally categorised as sexually abnormal, irrespective of desire. I think that Foucault is right that our desire is internally traversed by sexuality, but I see no convincing reason to think that this is not also true of pleasures or bodies. I accept that desire is slightly more bound up with sexuality than are pleasures or bodies, but the difference seems to me too minor to allow bodies and pleasures to function as *points d'appui* in resisting sexuality.

Foucault also suggests that pleasure is superior to desire in that it can involve multiple subjects, whereas desire is attached to the singular subject. This strikes me as ontologically false: if pleasure can involve multiple participants, so too can desire. If two people can experience one and the same pleasure at the same time (which is dubious), then two or more people can equally experience the same desire at the same time.

Foucault's attack on desire separates him from his contemporaries, particularly Deleuze. While Deleuze is generally even more critical of psychoanalysis than Foucault is, Deleuze wants to retain the notion of desire from psychoanalysis, albeit transformed in the direction of escaping the narrow individual subject, and indeed criticises psychoanalysis for constraining the infinite proliferation of desire.

Deleuze recalls a conversation with Foucault about desire and pleasure the last time the two saw each other.[55] Foucault explained his antipathy to the word desire, apologetically, knowing that the concept is key to Deleuze's thought. Foucault explained that he hated the word because he equated it either with lack (which is its Lacanian determination) or with the notion of repression of desire (that is, with the repressive hypothesis). He allows that in fact perhaps he calls 'pleasure' the very thing which Deleuze calls by the word 'desire'. Deleuze indeed does not think desire implies a lack. What he calls for is the continual production of new desires, which can explode the bounds of power, without any moment of constraining negativity. This avoids the trap Foucault is worried about by which our specific desires trap us in strategies of power, because Deleuze advocates continual innovation. Perhaps Foucault's position could be encapsulated by saying that desire is always specific to some extent: every desire has a specific object. By contrast, pleasure is not so specific, since it only has a specific object to the extent that it is attached to a desire. However, this remains an objection only to specific desires: it is not enough to indict desire itself as such. It is not clear how we could possibly proceed without having desires, or even that Foucault wants us to do so.

I think Foucault's antipathy for desire amounts to little more than a personal preference for which no philosophical justification can be given. Rather, it is, I think, necessary to be critical about any use of either pleasures or desires, since both pleasure and desire can serve, as well as resist, power.

Foucault's opposition to desire leads in a particular direction, towards an enjoyment of pleasure without attachment. It is not clear, however, that this follows from his critique of sexuality. It perhaps requires additional premises.

Resisting Sex

Foucault's purpose here is to resist sex. He makes a particularly interesting comment in this regard in the 1978 interview, that he does not mean to oppose the struggle for sexual liberation, but rather to extend it, turning the struggle against sexuality itself, to produce a liberation not only from repression but from sex as well.[56] Why should we want to be liberated from sex, however? Foucault has shown how sex relates to power, but he also shows us that power is ubiquitous and inevitable, that power in itself is no bad thing. I will conclude this guidebook by exploring the practical implications of Foucault's position, in relation to various movements that have tried derive a practice from his thought.

Sex and Crime

A very controversial aspect of Foucault's position is its apparent implications in relation to sex and crime. For Foucault, 'liberation from sex' seemed to imply demanding the abolition of laws governing sexual crime. A liberation from the category of sex would mean no more distinction between what is sexual and what is non-sexual. Important for understanding Foucault's position here are remarks he makes in a 1977 interview with Bernard-Henri Lévy. Foucault suggests, though he avers that this is only a suggestion, that children should be allowed to have polymorphous relationships with everything.[57] That is, liberation from sex means that children would no longer be banned from having sex, or, at least, what they are and are not allowed to do should not be governed by the category of sex. This does not mean everything is to be permitted then, only that whether it is sexual or not will not form the basis of the distinction. It does not therefore imply a licence to abuse children, for example.

This issue of rape is raised explicitly in another 1977 discussion, this one involving five participants, in which Foucault takes a leading role, alongside prominent English anti-psychiatrist David Cooper. Foucault had at this time recently been asked to give advice to a French government commission for the reform of the laws on sex. Foucault recommends the end of censorship of sexual material, but is less clear on the implications of his position regarding rape. The lack of clarity means that Foucault does not say definitively either way, but it is quite clear that he tends towards the abolition of rape as a specific crime, since the notion of sex is in effect contained within it. Where children are concerned, Foucault is on the side of reducing things to consent, although he is suspicious of that notion too because of his general suspicion of juridical notions.[58] That is, there is for him no specific problem of children and sex – the problem is one of rape.[59] The problem of rape is more intractable. Foucault's suggestion, which he perseveres with tentatively, is to assimilate rape to assault, that is, to remove the specifically sexual component of rape from the consideration of the crime, while still recognising it as criminal. The women participating in the discussion in particular disagree with Foucault on this point, declaring that rape is a special crime different in nature to assault, because more traumatic. But Foucault is sceptical of arguments from trauma, precisely because he believes the device of sexuality has the capacity to determine what is experienced as traumatic. That is, the peculiar trauma experienced by rape victims might only occur because rape is culturally constructed as a different kind of violation from other assaults. Foucault's final recommendation to government was more modest than the positions he suggests in this discussion: apparently he suggested a lowering of the age of consent to thirteen at the youngest, hardly a carte blanche for paedophilia.[60]

Feminism

David Macey notes that Foucault appears surprisingly ignorant of feminist concerns in his attitude to rape.[61] He does indeed seem to have little knowledge of or engagement with feminism, a naïvety that has itself drawn criticism from feminists. An important dimension of this is Foucault's uneasy relationship with the pre-eminent feminist philosopher of his time, Simone de Beauvoir. It is clear that Foucault did not care for Beauvoir, though it is less clear why. As multiple feminist authors have noted subsequently, Beauvoir's position is to some extent similar to Foucault's, in particular in her position that people have the role of 'woman' foisted on them by power. Foucault's hostility to Beauvoir would not seem to relate to her feminism, but rather to her personal and philosophical adherence to the pre-eminent French philosopher of the time, the existentialist Jean-Paul Sartre, and to the severe criticism levelled by Sartre's camp, including by Beauvoir herself in a satirical novel, at Foucault in the 1960s. The controversy between Foucault and Sartre was around Foucault's rejection of humanism (and with it the central emphasis on the importance of the conscious individual) and Marxism. This spat is indeed based on substantial theoretical differences, but I think may have blinded Foucault to points of similarity with Beauvoir's work on the questions of sex and sexuality, where Beauvoir, like Foucault, criticises purely biological, psychoanalytical and Marxist approaches.

Foucault has attracted some disapprobation from feminists for ignoring women's specific position in most of his works. Despite his lack of engagement with feminism, however, this hostility is dwarfed by the enormous influence his thought has had on feminism. *The Will to Knowledge* is perhaps the most influential single text for the development of what is called 'third wave feminism', the form of feminism that predominates today, and began in the 1980s.

The Will to Knowledge is the only of Foucault's books that deals with women specifically, as a group: women, as we have seen, are for him the particular target of one of the four great strategies of sexuality. His claims about the hysterisation of women were hardly news to feminists, however, and it is other aspects of the book that have influenced feminism.

Feminists have used ideas from *The Will to Knowledge* to combat two tendencies within feminism. One is a tendency to see women's condition in society as marked primarily by repression by 'patriarchal' power. This negative model became increasingly inadequate as the women's movement won rights within the juridical framework and the forms of difficulty women faced became less cases of overt discrimination, and more ones of covert power that worked to make women think of themselves in a certain way. *The Will to Knowledge* of course provides very clear criticisms of the limitations of conceiving politics as a question of legal rights. Indeed, to a large extent Foucault's reconception of power tallied with insights already widely held in the feminist movement, such as that 'the personal is political'. Previously this had been understood in terms of personal relationships replicating and/or being simply the local effect of a monolithic patriarchal power, but now Foucault's account of the complexity of power relations allowed new analyses.

Relatedly, another tendency of feminism, particularly in its previous, 'second wave', was towards 'gender essentialism'. That is, feminists tended to hold the view that men and women were intrinsically different, with women having superior innate capacities towards nurturing, cooperation, etc., in contrast to the aggressive tendencies of men. In this relation, Foucault's critique of sex proved influential.

The most prominent feminist with a Foucauldian orientation is Judith Butler. Indeed, Butler is arguably the most prominent feminist thinker of the last twenty years in any category. She took up Foucault's refusal to distinguish between an invariant biological sex and a culturally variable sexuality, and applied it to the distinction in feminist theory between supposedly biologically determined sex (male/female) and culturally variable 'gender'. Butler's Foucauldian gesture is to claim that the very notion of a biological male/female division is, like the idea of the biological category of sex, a cultural innovation.[62] That is, she argues that sex in the sense of the difference between men and women is also a historical construct occasioned by power relations that we need to get rid of. The reasons for wanting to get rid of it for feminists are: (1) that it stigmatises people who do not fit neatly into the division of the sexes (for example, women with what are seen as 'male traits' – but everyone can be said to fall foul of this at some point in their lives); (2) that it is a binary division created for the subjugation of women; (3) that any form of categorisation produced by power is limiting and thus is objectionable.

While this position does indeed mirror the main thesis of *The Will to Knowledge*, it is not clear from that book that Foucault would endorse such a position. It is not immediately obvious that any of his remarks in *The Will to Knowledge* about 'sex' refer to the difference between men and women. Rather, he seems primarily to use the word either as a shorthand for sexual intercourse, or in the French sense to refer to genitalia. However, Foucault elsewhere seems to make clear that he did intend his thesis about sex to apply to the male/female sex distinction, namely in his introduction to *Herculine Barbin, Being the Recently Discovered Memoirs of a Nineteenth-Century French Hermaphrodite*.

This book is the autobiography of a person of indistinct biological sex. Male medical specialists had determined that this intersex person was male, and she was forced to live under a male identity she did not accept. Ultimately, she took her own life. Such cases are of great importance to efforts to subvert the male/female distinction, because they show that this binary distinction is imposed on what is in fact, biologically, a continuum with a significant proportion of people finding themselves in between the two categories biologically. It also indicates the terrible consequences of this imposition.

Foucault was responsible for discovering these memoirs and having them published. In an introduction he provides to Barbin's text, Foucault asserts that the modern European notion of a biological 'true sex' is a recent invention. Previously, hermaphroditism was a legally acknowledged status that was neither male nor female, although there was a requirement for (a) a choice by a guardian as to what sex the child would be assigned during childhood followed by (b) a free choice by the hermaphrodite themselves as to which of the two sexes they would apply to themselves on reaching adulthood. This last decision was immutable, according to Foucault, and had to be retained throughout life.

Interestingly, this situation would seem to have been partially restored in the West since Foucault's time, more or less, and indeed one is now always allowed technically to change sex, both legally and anatomically. Until recently, however, this was not the case: during the nineteenth century, in particular, science did not allow that there were ultimately interstitial cases in relation to sex about which arbitrary choices needed to be made. Rather, the guiding principle was that there was a true sex lurking behind the sometimes confused anatomical evidence that needed to be discovered. As Foucault notes, things have moved on from the biology of the nineteenth century where the possibility of genetic conditions that were intersex was disallowed. From the point of view of contemporary genetics, most people either have a double X chromosome (in which case they are genetically female) or one X and one Y (in which case they are genetically male). Some intersex people exhibit an organic sex that is at variance with their genetic sex – hence are susceptible to a contemporary variant of the 'true biological sex' argument – but more than a few cases of hermaphroditism result from other chromosomal arrangements, meaning that genetics cannot be a basis for asserting that there are only two sexes exhibited by all individuals.

Foucault argues that the notion of true sex lingers, however. While he allows that we no longer see deviations from the norms as crimes against nature, he asserts that we continue to focus on normal, stereotypical cases: the powerful man and the submissive woman, with everything else worthy of less attention, seen as 'erroneous'. Foucault links this to the question of the 'truth of sex' in the very terms explored in *The Will to Knowledge*. The seamless way he does this indeed seems to imply that this was a connotation of his approach all along, that when he speaks about sex as produced by sexuality, and sex as what determines our identity, he means this to include the male/female distinction.

Important also about *The Will to Knowledge* for feminists is Foucault's focus on the body. Feminists have a longstanding interest in the question of the body for several reasons: the difference between men and women is typically seen as rooted in the physical, for one thing, but also because femininity has historically been associated with the body, while masculinity has been associated with the mind.

Actually, the feminist reception of Foucault goes much further than Foucault does in relation to the body. He, as we have seen, effectively puts sex on the side of the artificial construction and the body on the side of the real. Foucauldian feminists for the most part refuse to make any such distinction, and tend to see everything as culturally constructed, including the body itself. Accordingly, the body for them is seen as a 'text', which they can read in different ways.[63] This feminist understanding of Foucault's position on the body seems to infer from the fact that he thinks that discourse plays a role in constituting the body, that he must see the body as essentially discursive. But actually I think his point is more profound than this: discourse affects the body as it is ordinarily understood, in its material existence. This is seen particularly clearly in the above quote from an interview about the material penetration of the body by power. Ideas and language change the material body itself. For example, one could point out that the way we eat and the way we move, which both have material effects on the body, on its development and being, are affected profoundly by discourse.

Similarly, various feminist interpretations of the bodies and pleasures passage have been put forward with baroque explanations of its onto-logical meaning. Several feminist interpreters have taken bodies and pleasures here to be of the same order as sex itself, that is, concepts constructed in a particular discourse. The implication here seems to be that if sex is an 'artificial unity', so are all other concepts. But it seems rather clear to me that Foucault's whole point in saying that sex is an artificial unity is to differentiate it from other kinds of unity. The body is not an artificial unity: it is an objective and practical unity which is given to us before any kind of discursive categorisation. The feminist interpretations of Foucault here are explicitly influenced by the use of Foucault's French contemporaries, Jacques Derrida and Lacan. Derrida's position is that all reality is essentially like language, such that it would make sense to describe the body, or anything else at all really, as a text. Foucault never makes any such argument, however, and seems content to be simply realist where many objects are concerns. Lacan would dispute that the body's unity is pre-discursive, since he argues that we as infants initially encounter our own bodies as a confusing mass of sensations over which we have little control, and that unity thus has to be constructed through a false identification of ourselves with objects in our visual field, with the resulting subjective structure being the basis on which we acquire language. This does not imply, however, that 'body' is simply another historically constructed category. Rather, it implies that 'body' is a universal construct that all subjects must produce in order to pass into motile, language-using adulthood (though doubtless not all children do this). What I think we should take from Derrida and Lacan, however, is a certain caution as to how much the body can operate as a fulcrum of resistance. It is true that when we read the word 'body' on the page, this has many connotations through which any attempt to think about using it for resistance must pass, as feminist readers of Foucault have tended to note.

Queer Theory

The other major locus of reception of Foucault's ideas about sex is in what is called 'queer theory'. Queer theory is even more strongly influ-enced by Foucault than third wave feminism is: it is founded almost exclusively on Foucault's work. Queer theory is a theoretical discourse that seeks to subvert standard discourses about homosexuality. That is, it displaces the study of homosexuality in the direction of a refusal of labels, following Foucault's position of resistance to sexual categories. This involves an identification as 'queer' rather than 'homosexual'. Where 'homosexual' is a label that attaches us to a certain fixed sexual identity, 'queer' is a label that signals a refusal of such an identity. 'Queerness' indeed implies a subversion not only of labels like 'gay' or 'straight', but also 'male' and 'female'. Queer theory overlaps significantly with Foucauldian-influenced feminism. Butler is clearly the predominant figure in contemporary queer theory to an even greater extent than she predominates in contemporary feminism.

This is not to say that queer theory follows Foucault entirely, even if it would not exist without the influence of Foucault. Butler's thought is decisively influenced by Foucault, but even owes more, I would argue, to the thought of Foucault's student Derrida, and the latter's 'deconstructive' approach, which opposes all binary distinctions in thought in favour of the recognition of ambiguity, and the use of old vocabularies 'under erasure'.

Queer theory is to homosexuality as third wave feminism is to femininity. Where third wave feminism tends to reject any stereotyped version of the feminine, queer theory rejects the self-conscious identification of homosexuals with their homosexuality. The gay movement initially worked via a 'reappropriation' of the notion of homosexuality, which Foucault discusses in *The Will to Knowledge*. Though the concept that homosexuality is a natural inclination was an invention of psychiatrists within the device of sexuality, used initially to categorise homosexuals as sick, it has been taken up as a badge of honour by homosexuals themselves, saying that since they have been 'born this way', they cannot be blamed and must be allowed to be as they are.

To attack this notion of an essentially homosexual nature is problematic, because it is deeply cherished by many as part of their identity, and because it seems to put us on the side of those homophobes who commonly nowadays allege that people choose to be gay, with the implication that it is then acceptable to vilify homosexuals for choosing to do what homophobes regard as sinful or unnatural. Foucault does not condemn the tactic of claiming that homosexuality is natural in order to claim equal rights for homosexuals. He indeed rather lauds it. However, his overall judgement is that, even in resisting their vilification and pathologisation in this way, homosexuals end up reinforcing the device of sexuality. Their resistance is integrated into the strategy of power. I would argue that we see this today with the increasing acceptance of homosexuality in a way that does not seem to challenge the basic power structures around sex, such its assimilation to the institution of marriage, and indeed ultimately fails to abolish homophobia. The fuller form of resistance is one that resists all such labels. It is not clear to me why we need to have a homosexual/heterosexual labelling system unless it is in order to exclude someone or something.

This is not to say that Foucault definitively claimed that there is no biological basis for homosexuality. He simply, deliberately makes no comment at all in any direction about whether there is a biological component in play here, for the very good reason that it is not his area of expertise. He moreover thinks it is irrelevant to what he is doing, which is the history of power-knowledge.[64]

Notes

1. Foucault, *Courage of Truth*, p. 30.
2. Marcuse, *Eros and Civilization*, p. 239.
3. Foucault, *Abnormal*, pp. 42, 236.
4. Deleuze and Guattari, *Anti-Oedipus*, pp. 117–18, 127, 381–2.
5. The English edition appeared in 1977, but in *Power*, the third volume of the *Essential Works* anthology in English, its reprinting carries a note that it 'first appeared in French in 1976' – Foucault, *Power*, p. 110.
6. Defert, '« Je crois au temps . . . »: Daniel Defert légataire des manuscrits de Michel Foucault', p. 4.
7. Foucault, *Power/Knowledge*, p. 183.
8. Foucault, *Power/Knowledge*, pp. 183–4.
9. Foucault, *Power/Knowledge*, p. 185.
10. Foucault, *Aesthetics, Method, and Epistemology*, p. 370/Foucault, *Dits et écrits* II, p. 136.
11. See Megill, 'The Reception of Foucault by Historians'. Megill in fact shows that Foucault was initially ignored by historians, who then found he was becoming so important they had to confront him (by complaining about his use of facts), before accepting him (or, rather, assimilating his conclusions, while leaving his method to one side).
12. Foucault, *Discipline and Punish*, p. 31.
13. Hurley's translation of this sentence has an unusual number of small inaccuracies. He misses the entire part about functioning and *raisons*

d'être out; translates *determiner* as 'define' rather than 'determine' (implying that we have to say what it is on our own account, rather than find out by investigating); translates *il s'agit de* as 'the object is', when it is less definite, meaning simply that this is what our task is about, rather than that it is our singular objective; and translates *chez nous* as 'in our part of the world', a phrase that carries a much more geographic connotation than Foucault's and leaves the reader wondering (or at least it left me wondering, before I looked at the French) whether this 'part of the world' was France or Europe, where Foucault's phrasing refers only to 'us', a more clearly ambiguous term. Readers may question my leaving *raisons d'être* in French, but I think the French phrase is a more common formulation to find in English than the translated 'reasons for being'.

14. In French, Foucault repeats the phrase 'il se peut bien' here, which is translated differently by Hurley each time.

15. Beer, *Michel Foucault: Form and Power*, p. 3.

16. Beer, *Michel Foucault: Form and Power*, p. 2.

17. Hurley calls it a 'schism', but Foucault says *scission* rather than *schisme*. I suspect that Hurley chooses 'schism' precisely because the word has religious connotations, but the connotation of that word is strictly speaking inaccurate, since 'schism' in Christian terminology refers to a organisational split without significant doctrinal divergence, whereas from the Catholic perspective the Protestant Reformation is a heresy, a more substantial and less forgivable divergence.

18. Foucault, *Abnormal*, p. 184.

19. *My Secret Life* is an enormous, anonymous work of Victorian erotica, couched as a confessional. It provides a singularly important source for Marcus's *Other Victorians*.

20. Foucault, *Abnormal*, p. 292.

21. I use this example because it is one Foucault himself used in a much earlier interview of a fundamental reality that can be discovered; Foucault, *Dits et écrits* I, p. 515.

22. Beer (*Michel Foucault: Form and Power*, p. 67) argues that this 'is undoubtedly a reference to Reich's ideas'. I do doubt this, however: Beer's evidence is that Reich links the focus on reproduction to fascism, which Foucault does not.

23. Beer, *Michel Foucault: Form and Power*, pp. 32–3.

24. Foucault, *Dits et écrits* II, p. 552.

25. Foucault, *Ethics*, p. 259.

26. Foucault, 'Sexuality and Power', p. 117.
27. It is also noteworthy that the formulation mirrors rather Louis Althusser's formulation at the end of his 1970 essay on ideology, 'Ideology and Ideological State Apparatuses', that we simultaneously subject ourselves and are subjected. Interestingly, Althusser sees subjectivity as something which is imposed on pre-existing individuals, where Foucault sees both subjectivity and individuality as contingent.
28. Foucault, *Dits et écrits* III, p. 231; Foucault, *Power/Knowledge*, p. 187.
29. Foucault, *Discipline and Punish*, pp. 26–7.
30. Foucault, *Society Must Be Defended*, pp. 27, 29.
31. Hurley translates this as an 'analytics' of power. This is certainly a more usual translation. My reason for preferring 'analytic of power' is that it is similar to the usual translation of Heidegger's problematic in *Being and Time* as the 'analytic of Dasein', a similarity found in the French but lost in Hurley's translation.
32. Foucault, *Ethics*, p. 167; see also Kelly, *The Political Philosophy of Michel Foucault*, p. 107.
33. Kelly, *The Political Philosophy of Michel Foucault*, p. 36.
34. Foucault, *Dits et écrits* I, p. 514.
35. Foucault, *Power*, p. 341.
36. Habermas, *Philosophical Discourse of Modernity*, p. 276.
37. Marcuse, *Eros and Civilization*, p. 35.
38. Foucault, *Abnormal*, p. 200.
39. Foucault, *Power/Knowledge*, p. 219.
40. Foucault, *Politics, Philosophy, Culture*, p. 116.
41. Hurley renders *faire mourir* as '*take* life' rather than literally as '*make* die', which makes sense since in French *faire mourir* is a standard idiom, whereas it sounds odd in English, but the translation loses the starkness of Foucault's contrast between making live and making die.
42. Hurley here inexplicably translates *bio-politique* as 'bio-power' and even more inexplicably *pouvoir-savoir* as 'knowledge-power'.
43. Foucault, *Dits et écrits* III, p. 549 (in English as 'Sexuality and Power', p. 125); Foucault, *Dits et écrits* III, p. 561.
44. See Lemke, *Biopolitics: An Advanced Introduction*.
45. Foucault, *Security, Territory, Population*, p. 111.
46. Rabinow and Rose, 'Biopower Today', p. 208.
47. Foucault, *Power/Knowledge*, p. 190.
48. Foucault, *Power/Knowledge*, p. 186.
49. Deleuze, 'Desire and Pleasure', p. 186; Sylvère Lotringer also takes this

line in his introduction to Baudrillard's *Forget Foucault* (p. 18) – though it
is possible he got the idea from Deleuze.

50. Foucault, *Dits et écrits* II, p. 75.
51. Cf. Foucault, *Ethics*, p. 201.
52. Foucault, 'The Gay Science', p. 389.
53. Foucault, *Dits et écrits* III, p. 527.
54. Foucault, 'The Gay Science', p. 389.
55. Deleuze, 'Desire and Pleasure', p. 189.
56. Foucault, 'The Gay Science', p. 388.
57. Foucault, *Politics, Philosophy, Culture*, p. 117.
58. Foucault, *Politics, Philosophy, Culture*, p. 285.
59. Foucault, *Politics, Philosophy, Culture*, p. 289.
60. Foucault, 'The Gay Science', p. 402.
61. Macey, *The Lives of Michel Foucault*, p. 374.
62. Butler, *Gender Trouble*, p. 7.
63. See Judith Butler, *Bodies that Matter*; Susan Bordo, 'The Body and the
    Reproduction of Femininity: A Feminist Appropriation of Foucault';
    Jana Sawicki, *Disciplining Foucault*.
64. Foucault, *Politics, Philosophy, Culture*, p. 288.

3. Study Resources

Glossary

This section provides brief definitions of key terms used in *The Will to Knowledge*.

apparatus/device/deployment
see dispositif

dispositif
Discussing the notion of *dispositif* in *The Will to Knowledge* shortly after the book's publication, Foucault defines it as 'the network we can establish between' the elements of 'a resolutely heterogeneous ensemble, comprising discourses, institutions, architectural arrangements, regulatory decisions, laws, administrative measures, scientific statements, philosophical, moral and philanthropic propositions'.[1] So, it is a combination of discursive and non-discursive elements. The elements that comprise it function in a specific way within a given *dispositif*. The *dispositif* itself performs an overall function in a strategic situation.

The main difficulty with this word is not to understand its meaning, but to translate it. The noun *dispositif* in French occurs in two contexts. The first is law, where its English cognate, 'dispositive', is also found. Here it refers to dispositions of law. The second is mechanics, where it means the plan according to which things are made. Foucault, given his emphasis on deposing the model of law, clearly intends to use *dispositif* in the second sense, hence a literal translation as 'dispositive' would be inappropriate.

The word *dispositif* occurs 117 times in the original text of *The Will to*

---

[1] Foucault, *Power/Knowledge*, p. 194/ Foucault, *Dits et écrits* III, p. 299*.

Knowledge. Hurley translates this word of Foucault's with at least four different English terms: 'apparatus' (e.g. 55/74), 'deployment' (e.g. 23/33), 'device' (e.g. 45/62), 'machinery' (e.g. 32/45). On at least one occasion he uses different translations of *dispositif* in a single sentence (68/91, first as 'machinery' and then as 'deployment'). I regard this in itself as problematic: the same translation ought to be used in all instances, since it is clearly a core concept of Foucault's here, and there is no evidence that Foucault is using it in multiple different senses.

The translation as 'apparatus' is popular among translators of Foucault. In *Psychiatric Power*, for example, Graham Burchell translates *dispositif* uniformly as 'apparatus'. Most often, in English translations of Foucault, 'apparatus' corresponds to *dispositif* in the original. However, this is not always the case. Hurley does not reserve 'apparatus' for *dispositif* – he also uses it for *appareillage* (e.g. 23/33), and *appareil* (e.g. 55/74) – and other translators do similarly. I dislike the use of 'apparatus' for *dispositif* , which I prefer to be used for its French cognate, *appareil*, a word Foucault also uses. The major threat of confusion here comes from the influential use of *appareil* by Louis Althusser, translated into English as 'apparatus', most notably in his phrase 'Ideological State Apparatus'. To use 'apparatus' for Foucault's *dispositif* makes it seem like he is referencing Althusser where he is not.

There is more to be said in this connection too: *dispositif* in Althusser contrasts with *appareil*, with the former referring to something conceptual, and the latter to something institutional. The distinction between 'apparatus' and 'device' in English I think works in a similar way: while either thing is of course literally material, 'device' is much more usually used to refer to something immaterial (a 'dramatic device', for example) than is 'apparatus'. Foucault's choice of *dispositif* here rather than *appareil* similarly goes in this direction. Yes, for Foucault a *dispositif* encompasses both material and immaterial components, but it is important that he does not call it an *appareil*.

'Deployment' is Hurley's preferred translation of *dispositif.* This is an idiosyncratic choice. 'Deployment' implies that there is someone doing the deploying and a process of deployment, when neither is the case.

The translation as 'device' is thus my preferred one. It is literal, lacks any other obvious French correlate, and hence avoids confusion. I acknowledge that no translator of Foucault shares my enthusiasm for this translation, but I do not know why. There is a trend these days to use the French word untranslated in English-language texts, but I do not see any need for this. Admittedly, 'device' causes some confusion in relation to Hurley's translation, since Hurley uses the word 'device' to translate *appareil* on occasion (e.g. 34/47).

There are two significant secondary texts by prominent philosophers which ask the question 'What is a *dispositif*?' in relation to Foucault's thought, taking this question verbatim as their title. One is by Gilles Deleuze, the other by Giorgio Agamben. Both treatments are typically idiosyncratic. Deleuze's piece is a very brief reading of Foucault's entire oeuvre in Deleuzian terms, using the notion of *dispositif* to connect Foucault to Delcuze's own machinic ontology. The English translation of this text renders *dispositif* as 'apparatus'. Agamben, also using 'apparatus' in the English translation, produces a characteristic philological analysis, linking Foucault's notion tenuously to Hegel and Christian theology.

power-knowledge

Foucault coined this phrase at least as early as 1972.[2] It is sometimes taken to be the signature concept of Foucault's genealogical thought, though he only uses it five times in each of the books from this period of his work, *The Will to Knowledge* and *Discipline and Punish*. *The Will to Knowledge* seems to be the last time Foucault uses it at all. He abandons it later in favour of the concept of 'governmentality'.

The notion of 'power-knowledge' is sometimes presented as Foucault's alternative to the Marxist understanding of knowledge as 'ideology'.[3] A conventional Marxist view of ideology had grown up by Foucault's day by which 'ideology' was used to refer to what was taken to be a false image of reality which class societies produced. Marxism counterposed itself to this image, posing as the final true representation of reality free from ideology. This account was questioned by Althusser, who articulated his own account of ideology by which any knowledge always involved some kind of distortion of reality, Marxism included.

It is clear enough that Foucault would have no truck with the conventional Marxist view, by which power distorts knowledge and Marxism frees knowledge from power. Althusser's view, however, is close to Foucault's own. Foucault, however, refuses resolutely to utilise the word 'ideology'. Why? Two simple reasons are that Foucault does not want to risk any association with the conventional Marxist notion, and that,

---

[2] Foucault, *Dits et écrits* II, p. 390.
[3] This is how Foucault explicitly presents it at *Power*, p. 87.

unlike Althusser, he has no reason to use a Marxist phrase since Foucault is not a Marxist. Still, it indicates a difference between Foucault and Althusser that is more substantive. Althusser maintained in his Marxism a need to assert the priority of the economic 'infrastructure' over 'super-structural' knowledge, albeit that his maintenance of this principle dissolved over the course of his career. For Foucault, unlike for Marxism, there is no hierarchy between knowledge and power, or indeed between any such orders. Where Marxists think of knowledge (at least non-Marxist knowledge) as being the product of a particular socio-economic order, Foucault simply views knowledge as always having relations with power, and vice versa, such that either knowledge or power only ever exists in practice in combination with the other, in a particular 'power-knowledge' configuration.[4] This concept is thus emblematic of the change in Foucault's work of the 1970s compared with his work of the mid- to late 1960s: in the earlier work, he approached knowledge by bracketing other concerns, whereas now he insists that knowledge cannot be understood except as correlative to power. He will later come to understand this approach as inadequate in turn because there are other things (most importantly subjectivity) that it does not include, with the concept of governmentality that he develops later being in part an attempt to address this deficiency.

psychiatry

The branch of medicine dealing with the mind. Not to be confused with 'psychology' (the academic study of the mind) or 'psychoanalysis' (see below), though at various times these three have been close to synony-mous in practice.

psychoanalysis

Theory of mind and psychotherapeutic technique propounded originally by Sigmund Freud. The basic insight of the psychoanalytic account of the mind is the notion of the unconscious as the most important compo-nent of the psyche. On this basis, Freud produced an account of neurotic illness as due to the 'repression' of unpalatable unconscious inclinations. The technique of psychoanalysis attempted to uncover these through getting patients to talk at length about the past and dreams, and thus to

---

[4] In this, Foucault follows his sometime mentor Louis Althusser, who, though a Marxist, thought that all knowledge, even Marxism, was ideological.

deal with them. Those who practise this technique are called 'psycho-analysts'.

sex (*sexe*)

In English, the word 'sex' has two meanings, but its French cognate, *sexe*, has three. Hence, in reading *The Will to Knowledge* in English, one ought to understand 'sex' as connoting all three meanings implied in French. The meanings in English are firstly, its original meaning, the categorisation of things as male or female, what is often today called 'gender'. The word in English has acquired a second meaning, which has become dominant, namely coitus. Here, sex is shorthand for 'sexual intercourse', which was so-called because it was intercourse between the sexes, between a man and a woman. Today, however, we can talk about a man having sex with another man. What is this paradoxical object 'sex' that has crept in? What does this thing refer to? Not something a man does with a woman, but something one person does with another person, involving their bodies, specifically one imagines involving their sexual organs. Foucault's claim is that no such notion existed until a few hundred years ago, that there was no such category of the 'sexual'. Similar acts may have existed, but they were not all lumped together in the same way. Rather, they were lumped together in Christian thinking as 'carnal' acts, acts of the flesh, but this was a larger category than the sexual. The third meaning, present in French and also lumped into this category from Foucault's point of view, are the genitalia. That is, in French, *sexe* can refer to a penis or a vagina as well as to the things 'sex' refers to in English, making it an even more heterogeneous category than we are used to.

Further Reading

Works by Foucault

Some texts by Foucault provide useful additional reading for understanding *The Will to Knowledge*. The most relevant of his books to read are those of the same period. I list books here in order of relevance. It is worth bearing in mind that only the first three I list here were ever intended by Foucault to be published as books; the rest of these are publications of lecture series that he never intended for publication and hence cannot be said to have the same finality as his books. As often with Foucault, some of the most useful things to read by him are not full books at all, but shorter pieces and interviews he gave. I refer to such material in a separate list below the books.

Discipline and Punish, trans. Alan Sheridan (London: Allen Lane, 1977). Originally published as *Surveiller et punir* (Paris: Gallimard, 1975).

> Foucault's first full-scale genealogy, *Discipline and Punish* focuses on the emergence of the contemporary prison system in the eighteenth and nineteenth centuries. More generally, it provides a genealogical study of the form of power that Foucault refers to as disciplinary. Since this is one element for him of the formation of biopower which leads to the prominence of the device of sexuality, this is an important adjunct to the genealogy of sexuality.

The Use of Pleasure, vol. 2 of *The History of Sexuality*, trans. Robert Hurley (New York: Pantheon, 1985). Originally published as *L'Usage des plaisirs* (Paris: Gallimard, 1984).

The Care of the Self, vol. 3 of *The History of Sexuality*, trans. Robert Hurley (New York: Pantheon, 1986). Originally published as *Le Souci de soi* (Paris: Gallimard, 1984).

> The second and third volumes of *The History of Sexuality*, *The Use of Pleasure* and *The Care of the Self*, are also of interest of course, but do not help much in understanding *The Will to Knowledge*. From the point of view of the first volume of *The History of Sexuality*, the other two volumes serve only to confirm how dissimilar contemporary sexuality is from what existed in ancient Greek and Roman societies. Of course, if one wants to understand the entire history of sexuality, they are indispensable.

Society Must Be Defended, trans. David Macey (New York: Picador, 2003). Originally published as *Il faut défendre la société* (Paris: Gallimard, 1997).

> *Society Must Be Defended* is a course of lectures delivered by Foucault at the beginning of 1976. Though *The Will to Knowledge* appeared later, at the end of 1976, it seems to sit between the lectures of 1975, *Abnormal* and these 1976 lectures. While *Abnormal* includes much material on sexuality, *Society Must Be Defended* contains almost none. It is concerned more with power. The explicit theme of *Society Must Be Defended* is racism: it is a genealogy of racism. Foucault finds two kinds of historic racist discourse: one which criticises society as a form of war between groups, which he in fact wants to take up and develop in his reconception of power, and one which develops into part of the modern biopolitical state form. Accordingly, these

lectures conclude with an extensive consideration of biopolitics, and the function of racism within them. They are therefore useful in understanding Foucault's thinking about power and especially biopower in *The Will to Knowledge*.

Abnormal, trans. Graham Burchell (London: Verso, 2003). Originally published as *Les Anormaux* (Paris: Editions de Seuil/Gallimard, 1999).

Abnormal deals with what Foucault calls 'the power of normalisation', that is, the power that declares people to be abnormal in various ways. He talks about this power in *The Will to Knowledge*, but provides much more detail here. This power is here associated with both the criminal justice system and psychiatry: indeed, his first example is the crossover of these two institutions. Thus, the first part of the book effectively combines the concerns of *Psychiatric Power* with those of *Discipline and Punish*, looking at the intersection of psychiatry and punishment. There is also a strong theme of the examination of perversion and of sexuality. The book thus links together the *History of Madness* with *Discipline and Punish* and *The Will to Knowledge*. Abnormality is a kind of master concept that covers all of these studies, and shows Foucault's debt to Georges Canguilhem's study of *The Normal and the Pathological*. The final three lectures of *Abnormal* cover themes that are dealt with in *The Will to Knowledge*, though with substantial additional material. The preceding chapters, the seventh and eighth, provide a good deal of background material about Christian practices leading up to the invention of sexuality, which Foucault does not go into in *The Will to Knowledge*.

Psychiatric Power, trans. Graham Burchell (New York: Palgrave Macmillan, 2006). Originally published as *Le Pouvoir psychiatrique* (Paris: Gallimard, 2003).

The lectures on *Psychiatric Power* were given by Foucault at the end of 1973 and beginning of 1974, three years then before *The Will to Knowledge* appeared. At the beginning of these lectures (p. 4), Foucault already expounds a version of the view of power found in *The Will to Knowledge*. There is indeed an entire axis of the history of sexuality of *The Will to Knowledge* which is in effect traced out in *Psychiatric Power*. It is no coincidence that the conclusion of *Psychiatric Power*, the final remarks of the last lecture, concern the invention by psychiatrists of what Foucault calls the 'sexual body'.

The Courage of Truth, trans. Graham Burchell (Basingstoke: Palgrave

Macmillan, 2011). Originally published as *Le Courage de la vérité* (Paris: Gallimard, 2008).

The newly published 1984 lecture series *The Courage of the Truth* is useful in providing some kind of connection between the second and third volumes of *The History of Sexuality* and the more contemporary ambit of *The Will to Knowledge*, indicating the transformation of the will to knowledge that occurred in between antiquity and modernity.

Shorter Pieces

Power/Knowledge, ed. Colin Gordon (Brighton: Harvester, 1980).

The earliest anthology of Foucault's interviews and shorter writings, this is still perhaps the best, and certainly is so for readers of *The Will to Knowledge*. Its last two pieces, 'The History of Sexuality' and 'The Confession of the Flesh', are both interviews dealing with *The Will to Knowledge*. The piece 'Two Lectures' here comprises the first two chapters of *Society Must Be Defended*, which are also very relevant. 'Truth and Power' and 'Power and Strategies' are both from 1977 and deal with questions around power, both with particular attention to Marxism and its concerns.

'The Subject and Power' (1982).

A piece of extraordinary importance, where Foucault gives his clearest views on the concept of power outside of *The Will to Knowledge*. It has been reprinted in multiple places, but perhaps the most widely available source is the third volume of the *Essential Works* collection, entitled *Power*.

Politics, Philosophy, Culture, ed. Lawrence D. Kitzman (New York: Routledge, 1988).

This is also a very relevant collection. The most relevant pieces are 'Power and Sex' and 'Confinement, Psychiatry, Prison'. In addition to these two, there are two sections of the book dedicated to sexuality, from pages 227–306. The first of these sections, 'The Ethics of Sexuality', deals with Foucault's later reflections on ancient sexuality; the second, 'The Politics of Sexuality', contains two interviews, the first, 'Sexual Morality and the Law', indicating Foucault's views about paedophilia, and the second, 'Sexual Choice, Sexual Act', including his views concerning homosexuality.

'Introduction', *Herculine Barbin, Being the Recently Discovered Memoirs of a Nineteenth-Century French Hermaphrodite* (New York: Pantheon, 1980).

Less than eleven pages in length, and really only the first four dealing with the crucial theoretical questions, Foucault's introduction to this volume is nonetheless an important a supplement to *The Will to Knowledge* that extends its analysis to the question of the male/female sexual distinction.

Dits et écrits, 4 vols (Paris: Gallimard, 1994).

In French, almost all Foucault's interviews and shorter writings are collected in this single multi-volume French collection. Unfortunately, this collected edition has not been translated into English. Rather, English readers are forced to contend with an array of anthologies, the two most relevant of which I have just listed, with often overlapping selections, and much remains untranslated.

I give page references in endnotes above to *Dits et écrits* in its original four-volume edition. It has since been reissued with the same material bound in two volumes, with accordingly altered paginations.

Selected Secondary Works

There are dozens of books about Foucault's thought. Most of these in their way are useful to understanding the overall context of *The Will to Knowledge*, and most have some things to say about that book specifically; however, I here list a few books of particular interest.

Armstrong, Timothy J. (ed.), *Michel Foucault: Philosopher* (Hemel Hempstead: Harvester Wheatsheaf, 1992).

A particularly good collection of papers on Foucault by his contemporaries.

Beer, Dan, *Michel Foucault: Form and Power* (Oxford: European Humanities Research Centre, 2002).

Beer's book is the only other book than this one to date that is specifically about Foucault's *Will to Knowledge*. Beer's effort is rather more scholarly than this book: all quotations from Foucault and other French sources appear untranslated in the original French, and there is a great deal of attention to Foucault's literary style, his choice of words, and even his syntax. Beer explores the content of *The Will to Knowledge* through tangential literary comparisons with its source materials or literature that bears on periods and themes under discussion. In short, this is nothing like a guidebook. Though it has much of interest to anyone who wants to understand the book in depth, I am moreover not sure that it represents Foucault's position accurately.

Davidson, Arnold I., *The Emergence of Sexuality: Historical Epistemology and the Formation of Concepts* (Cambridge, MA: Harvard University Press, 2001).

This book is a collection of essays by Davidson, not all of which are explicitly about Foucault, but as a whole it provides a number of useful tangents from *The Will to Knowledge*. 'Sex and the Emergence of Sexuality' in particular is a supplement to the historical material in Foucault's book. Davidson's appendix is also particularly interesting, giving a brief account of Foucault's relation to psychoanalysis.

Deleuze, Gilles, *Foucault*, trans. Seán Hand (London: Athlone, 1988).

The author of this book was a major philosopher in his own right, and a friend of Foucault's. This book has the advantage then of having an extraordinarily qualified author. It is the only book written by a big-name philosopher about Foucault, and the only book that Deleuze wrote about a contemporary of his. I think it is clearly the best book about Foucault's thought, although, as is typical of Deleuze's work on other thinkers, it is idiosyncratic, to some extent reflecting Deleuze's own position more than Foucault's. This book is particularly thorough on epistemological/methodological questions, and also contains a relevant chapter on power.

Kelly, Mark G. E., *The Political Philosophy of Michel Foucault* (New York: Routledge, 2009).

My previous book on Foucault concentrates specifically on the political and philosophical angles to his work. It thus has quite a lot to say about the political and philosophical dimension of *The Will to Knowledge*, though little to say about the historical account of sexuality itself. The first chapter, 'Epistemology', provides some background to Foucault's method in terms of the development of his epistemology. The second chapter, 'Power I', deals with his earlier views on power, including those in *Will to Knowledge*. The third chapter, 'Power II', deals with Foucault's later extension of his account of power to incorporate the subject. The fourth chapter, 'Subjectivity', deals with Foucault's account of subjectivity, showing how the account of subjection found in *The Will to Knowledge* later fits into a fuller account. The fifth chapter,

'Resistance', is a largely speculative reading of the remarks on resistance in *The Will to Knowledge*. The sixth and seventh chapters deal with the stakes of philosophy for Foucault, and as such give an account of his purpose in writing his books.

Macey, David, *The Lives of Michel Foucault* (London: Hutchinson, 1993).

Macey, David, *Michel Foucault* (London: Reaktion Books, 2004).

The first of these books is the most comprehensive and best biography of Foucault. It is, however, enormous. For those with less time, looking for a biography on Foucault, the second of Macey's books offers an excellent potted version.

Mahon, Michael, *Foucault's Nietzschean Genealogy: Truth, Power, and the Subject* (Albany: SUNY Press, 1992).

A pointedly philosophical work on the influence of Nietzsche on Foucault.

Critical Works

There is no shortage of critical material on Foucault either. The seven-volume Routledge *Michel Foucault: Critical Assessments* series edited by Barry Smart contains a wealth of material. David Couzens Hoy (ed.), *Foucault: A Critical Reader* (Oxford: Blackwell, 1986) is noteworthy, particularly for its inclusion of Charles Taylor's essay 'Foucault on Freedom and Truth'. Jürgen Habermas's important critique of Foucault is most prominently found in his *The Philosophical Discourse of Modernity*, trans. Frederick Lawrence (Cambridge, MA: MIT Press, 1990). The key parts of this can also be found excerpted in the collection Michael Kelly (ed.), *Critique and Power: Recasting the Foucault/Habermas Debate* (Cambridge, MA: MIT Press).

Other Works Cited

Agamben, Giorgio, *Homo Sacer*, trans. Daniel Heller-Roazen (Stanford: Stanford University Press, 1998).

—, *What Is an Apparatus?*, trans. David Kishik and Stefan Pedatella (Stanford: Stanford University Press, 2009).

Althusser, Louis, 'Ideology and Ideological State Apparatuses', in *Lenin and Philosophy and Other Essays*, trans. Ben Brewster (London: New Left Books, 1971), pp. 127–93.

Bartky, Sandra Lee, '"Catch Me if You Can": Foucault on the Repressive Hypothesis', in *'Sympathy and Solidarity' and Other Essays* (Lanham, MD: Rowman and Littlefield, 2002), pp. 47–68.

Baudrillard, Jean, *Forget Foucault* (Los Angeles: Semiotext(e), 2007).

Bordo, Susan, 'The Body and the Reproduction of Femininity: A Feminist Appropriation of Foucault', in Alison M. Jaggar (ed.), *Gender / Body / Knowledge: Feminist Reconstructions of Being and Knowing* (Piscataway, NJ: Rutgers University Press, 1989), pp. 13–33.

Butler, Judith, *Gender Trouble* (New York: Routledge, 1990).

—, *Bodies that Matter* (New York: Routledge, 1993).

Defert, Daniel, '« Je crois au temps . . . »: Daniel Defert légataire des manuscrits de Michel Foucault', *Recto / Verso*, N° 1 (Juin 2007), pp. 1–7.

Deleuze, Gilles, 'What is a *dispositif*?', in *Michel Foucault: Philosopher*, trans. Timothy J. Armstrong (Hemel Hempstead: Harvester Wheatsheaf, 1992), pp. 159–68.

—, 'Desire and Pleasure', in Arnold I. Davidson (ed.), *Foucault and His Interlocutors* (Chicago: Chicago University Press, 1997), pp. 183–94.

Deleuze, Gilles and Félix Guattari, *Anti-Oedipus: Capitalism and Schizophrenia* (Minneapolis: University of Minnesota Press, 1983).

Dreyfus, Hubert and Paul Rabinow, *Michel Foucault: Beyond Structuralism and Hermeneutics* (Chicago: University of Chicago Press, 1983).

Eribon, Didier, *Michel Foucault* (Cambridge, MA: Harvard University Press).

Foucault, Michel, *Archaeology of Knowledge*, trans. Sheridan Smith (London: Routledge, 1989).

—, *Ethics*, vol. 1 of *Essential Works* (New York: New Press, 1997).

—, *Aesthetics, Method, and Epistemology* vol. 3 of *Essential Works* (New York: New Press, 1998).

—, 'Sexuality and Power', in Jeremy R. Carrette (ed.), *Religion and Culture* (New York: Routledge, 1999), pp. 115–30.

—, *Power*, vol. 3 of *Essential Works* (New York: New Press, 2001).

—, *Security, Territory, Population* (Basingstoke: Palgrave Macmillan, 2007).

—, 'The Gay Science', trans. Nicolae Morar and Daniel W. Smith, *Critical Inquiry*, vol. 37, no. 3 (Spring 2011), pp. 385–403.

Friedrich, Otto, 'France's Philosopher of Power', *Time*, 6 November 1981, pp. 147–8.

Lawrence, D. H., 'A propos of *Lady Chatterley's Lover*' (London: Mandrake, 1930).

Lemke, Thomas, *Biopolitics: An Advanced Introduction* (New York: New York University Press, 2011).

Marcuse, Herbert, *Eros and Civilization* (Boston, MA: Beacon, 1966).

—, *One-Dimensional Man* (Boston, MA: Beacon, 1991).

McWhorter, Ladelle, *Bodies and Pleasures: Foucault and the Politics of Sexual Normalization* (Bloomington: Indiana University Press, 1999).

Megill, Allan, 'The Reception of Foucault by Historians', *Journal of the History of Ideas*, vol. 48, no. 1 (Jan.–Mar. 1987), pp. 117–41.

Nietzsche, Friedrich, *On the Genealogy of Morality*, trans. Maudemarie Clark and Alan J. Swensen (Indianapolis: Hackett, 1998).

Patton, Paul, 'Taylor and Foucault on Power and Freedom', *Political Studies*, vol. 37 (1989), pp. 260–76.

—, 'Foucault's Subject of Power', in Jeremy Moss (ed.), *The Later Foucault: Politics and Philosophy* (London: Sage, 1998), pp. 64–77.

Rabinow, Paul and Nikolas Rose, 'Biopower Today', *BioSocieties*, vol. 1, no. 2 (2006), pp. 195 218.

Sawicki, Jana, *Disciplining Foucault* (New York: Routledge, 1991).

Van Ussel, Jos, *Geschiedenis van het seksuele probleem* (Amsterdam: Boom Koninklijke Uitgevers, 1968).

Answering Essay and Examination Questions

It is difficult to give a definitive guide to doing assignments on Foucault's book because of the number of different disciplines in which it is taught. What is expected of students in philosophy may be rather different from what is expected in, say, cultural studies. When in doubt, questions about how to approach your assessment tasks should always be directed to your teacher.

I have tried here to elaborate various dimensions of Foucault's work in this book: his use of terminology, the logic of his argument, the historical context in which he wrote, and the relation of his thought to that of other thinkers.

Different parts of my explanation will be relevant to different kinds of questions. It is worth warning you not to parrot material from this book: not only would that be plagiarism, but I have also given much more detail than would ever be needed in any given essay. My aim is to give all the information that you might need to do work on Foucault's book, but it does not follow logically from that that everything I say will be useable for any one reader.

Types of Question You Might Encounter
Questions about The History of Sexuality
Basic comprehension questions will often ask about specific elements of Foucault's historical account. For these, I advise simply reading the relevant part of this guidebook along with the relevant part of Foucault's

book. This guidebook has deliberately been laid out following the order of *The Will to Knowledge* to make it easier to find the part of it that is relevant.

Questions about Homosexuality and Gender

The Will to Knowledge is typically read in relation to queer theory and women's studies. While Foucault's book certainly does talk frequently about the situation of homosexuals and women in relation to sexuality, it is not entirely clear what the message of the book is for these groups. I discuss these issues at the very end of the second chapter above.

The Biopower / Biopolitics Question

With the increased interest in the concept of biopolitics in recent years, it is inevitable that readings of *The Will to Knowledge* often focus on this element. I have outlined the major competing notions of biopolitics to Foucault's when discussing his views above.

The Historical Question

Questions about the historicity of Foucault's work abound. These are of course most likely to be asked in courses taught in History departments.

One aspect of such a question is historiographical, asking what kind of history Foucault is doing, or whether what he is doing counts as history. Here, the reader must be referred to Foucault's essay 'Nietzsche, Genealogy, History', which explains the historiographical aspect of Foucault's genealogical method.

Another aspect of the question is simply factual, that is, whether what Foucault is saying is true. Some have criticised the factual accuracy of *The Will to Knowledge*, notably Sandra Lee Bartky in her essay '"Catch Me if You Can": Foucault on the Repressive Hypothesis', though her objections have less evidence behind them than Foucault's assertions do, and in any case mainly misunderstand Foucault. The important thing to note about Foucault here is how limited his claims are. He does not claim, for example, as Bartky thinks, that there has never been any sexual repression. His methodology is just to add to the well-known facts of sexual repression a new interpretation of other known facts to produce a new overall account.

The Power Question

Questions about Foucault's views on power require engagement with *The Will to Knowledge*. Fortunately, his views on power are contained within a small portion of the book, namely the first two chapters of Part Four. Unfortunately, these are very dense and require careful close reading. Additional reading of Foucault's shorter writing and interviews is invaluable in understanding his views on power, with 'The Subject and Power' being the most important, and the volume of *Essential Works* entitled *Power* and the *Power/Knowledge* collection each providing much that is useful. There is a significant secondary literature on this issue too, of which I particularly recommend Taylor's 'Foucault on Freedom and Truth', Paul Patton's response to that ('Taylor and Foucault on Power and Freedom'), and a later piece by Patton called 'Foucault's Subject of Power'. My earlier book on Foucault's political philosophy has two chapters on Foucault's conception of power that are probably the most extensive overview available, as well as providing many more secondary references.

The Psychoanalysis Question

Foucault's book sometimes crops up in relation to the critique of psychoanalysis, though rarely on its own – it would make more sense in the context of looking at the critique of psychiatry or psychoanalysis across several texts, either of Foucault's (i.e. *History of Madness, The Birth of the Clinic, Psychiatric Power*) or of other authors (e.g. British anti-psychiatry, Deleuze and Guattari's work). Foucault's remarks in relation to psychoanalysis occur in a few distinct places in the book. For a question of this kind, judicious use of the index of both Foucault's book and of this guidebook in identifying key passages is advised.

The Repressive Hypothesis Question

Questions about Foucault's book sometimes focus on the repressive hypothesis, that is, on defining it and saying how his position differs from it. The great difficulty with such questions is that his precise position is so ill understood that often the one assessing your answers will not understand Foucault's position well. Careful reading of this guidebook, and careful referencing to it, should ensure a correct response (you might disagree with my interpretation of Foucault, of course, but at least the use of this guidebook ought to provide you with something against which to clearly mark out your own interpretation). The relevant material is in Part One of *The Will to Knowledge* and in the corresponding section of this book.

Tips for Writing About Foucault

1. It is very important to a quality essay to show, both through references and through a sophistication of engagement, that you have read relevant secondary literature. The secondary literature on Foucault's book is not that great, either in terms of quantity or quality, but I attempt to give some good pointers for things to look at under 'Further Reading' above.

2. One general tip for writing about Foucault – or indeed any continental philosopher – is not to emulate his style. Foucault does not put things straightforwardly, and hardly ever references. This was tolerated in France among professors in Foucault's day. It is not tolerated among undergraduates – or even professors – in English-speaking universities today. You should aim at bringing clarity to Foucault's position by laying things out more simply and clearly than he does, and referencing fully. It is rare for students to reference too copiously – when in doubt, cite.

3. Doing all this is not easy. The main task in respect of Foucault's book in any essay is to pay close attention to what he is saying and not rely on glib characterisations of his position you may have picked up elsewhere. This is particularly true in the discipline of philosophy, but should be true in others. You should try to think in terms of the overall argument he is making, and reconstruct this, then put it clearly to your reader (namely, the one marking your assignment) and give evidence for your reading, using quotations and precise page references to support your case.

4. If you can read French well enough, then read Foucault in the original. If you cannot, be sure to check the relevant place of this guidebook to see if there is something problematic I note about the passage in the English translation you are referring to.

Index

Printed and bound by CPI Group (UK) Ltd, Croydon, CR0 4YY

03/02/2025

01830792-0003